D1664498

THE MYSTIQUE OF SĪGIRIYA

WHISPERS OF THE MIRROR WALL

THE MYSTIQUE OF SĪGIRIYA

WHISPERS OF THE MIRROR WALL

W. J. M. LOKUBANDARA

GODAGE INTERNATIONAL PUBLISHERS (PVT) LTD
SRI LANKA

© W. J. M. Lokubandara

Visual Concept & Editing
Patrick Ratnayake

First Published 2007

ISBN 978-955-30-0610-3

Photography
Patrick Ratnayake
Gamini Jayasinghe
Mahesh Prasantha
Upul Jayantha Ranepura
Nuwan Duminda

Cover design
Priyangika Kotalawala
Upul Jayantha Ranepura

Page setting
Priyangika Kotalawala
Thanoja Priyadarshani

Type setting
Hiranthi Lanka Gunawardana

Publication
Godage International Publishers (Pvt) Ltd.
Colombo, Sri Lanka.
E mail : godage@slt.lk www.godage.com

Printing
Tharanjee Printers
Maharagama, Sri Lanka.

DEDICATION

To
Malathi
The feminine ideal
of
the Sigiriya poets

ලැදී මන බන්ද්නා
පැහැබර සිනා රැස්නා
කතක්හී තොස්නා
මිණිඅකුසු හිස්හි ලයි ගන්නා

(Sigiri Graffiti - 306)

Translation

To have one's mind ensnared, being attached to her, by a damsel who is winsome on account of her radiant smile and who is pleasing, is (like unto) taking a jewelled hook of an elephant - driver and placing it on (one's own) head.

CONTENTS

ABOUT THIS BOOK 9-13

SIGIRI GEE SIRI -THE ENGLISH VERSION 15-18

THE SIGIRIYA POETRY AND THE AESTHETICS OF THE POPULAR POETIC TRADITION 21-28

ENFRAMING SIGIRI POETRY 29-35

SIGIRI Gī THE MIRROR WALL POEMS 37-38

ACKNOWLEDGEMENT 39

MAY THEIR IDENTITY REMAIN UNSOLVED FOR EVER! 41-55

FLOWERS IN THEIR HANDS - SYMBOLS OF LOVE 57-66

SONGS ON THE MIRROR WALL AT SIGIRIYA 69-80

THE COQUETTISH SMILE, THE SEEDS OF THE MELON 83-86

THE CHARM OF SIGIRI POETRY: REFLECTIONS ON THE MIND 89-94

TO LEAP FROM A PEAK 97-104

SUGGESTIVE SILENCE 107-119

FAME AND GLORY OF THE LION KING 121-125

THUS SHONE THE LAKE IN SPLENDOUR 127-132

THE FIVE HUNDRED DAMSELS OF SIGIRIYA 135-149

VIVIFICATION OF SONG THROUGH DIALOGUE 151-161

NECTAR OF SONG
The Sigiri Paintings and the Poets 163-166

ABOUT THIS BOOK

For those of us from the hills of Haputale who believed in a certain shade of politics in Sri Lanka, the 01st January 1977 was a memorable day. It was a ceremonial rally, presided over by our leader the late Hon. J.R.Jayewardene on his campaign trail. There was a massive crowd gathered on the grounds of the Sunday Fair at Diyatalawa. I was scheduled to speak and it was my political debut. A perfect greenhorn to the rough and ready game of politics, I had been nursed on gentler stuff as poetry. Standing up to face the crowd my mind went blank. I could see nothing, feel nothing and felt certain, could say nothing. Then out of the depths of that frightening void, almost subconscious memory, came a verse that escaped my frozen lips, like a bird from a cage.

"Topa vanavu himin
Himak etak notabai
Ukatali muhund pihinanu
Vani anda pilu gele gamana"

It was a lyric gem, a graffito from the mirror wall of the Lion Rock – *Sigiriya* – written by an unknown poet somewhere in the 8th century. As I subconsciously remembered the poem, an impromptu translation came to my mind.

"O fair one! Deep in sorrow and lamenting for your departed husband, aren't you like the blind man who waits to journey on the shoulders of the lame? The blind can walk yet not see. The lame can see yet not walk. Why be despondent on either side? *Let the blind carry the lame."*

I, who am poor, can go to parliament only on the wings of your vote. Thus did I appeal to them for mutual support. My leader, the late Hon. J.R.Jayewardene, responded warmly and in his pithy elegant manner remarked " When I heard Lokubandara speaking today, I thought of Sir D.B.Jayatilaka, my predecessor in Parliament from the Kelaniya seat,who was the first Leader of the House of the State Council. We must select educated, efficient people to lead the country after us. Although I had seen the Sigiri frescoes, this is the first time I heard these verses from the political platform. Haputale's future should be in the care of Lokubandara. And Lokubandara's future should be in the care of the people of Haputale."

And so it has been for the last three decades. May this book be my belated tribute to that unknown poet who led me across the centuries to hold my hand at that crucial moment in my life, and also to all those other anonymous poets who illuminated the mirror wall at the Lion Rock with their radiant poetry.

Literature has been my passion from childhood. My world of emotion extended its scope with the Sigiri poems. I, who was brought up on a staple of classical oriental poetry with the rich imagery of ***Kavsilumina,*** the polyphonic rhythms of ***Mayura Sandesa,*** the pure and elegantly simple cadenzas of ***Guttila,*** the fascinating music of ***Selalihini Sandesa*** and of course the deep sonorous splendour of Sanskrit prose along with the calm spiritual tone of Pali and the Vedic texts, responded on a different wavelength to the sensuality of the Sigiri verses.

Thus the Sigiri Graffiti added a new dimension to my mind, which I had never experienced earlier. It was a treasure house of poetic flavour that enlivened my heart. I was enraptured by the Sigiri poetry that depicted the best in Sinhala civilization.

As a school boy I had joined the trail-blazing mission of *Hela Havula,* and I was not satisfied with a mere study of the few Sigiri verses that were prescribed for the examination. Various treatises by Kumaratunga Munidasa always helped me in the study of Sinhala literature. Venturing upon this unfamiliar territory, I studied Paranavitana's monumental work not once but several times.

The Sigiri Rock, visited by our ancestors, throughout centuries, epitomizes the Sinhala nation as does the Lion on our National flag. It stands for the supremacy of determination, imagination, and creative ability; a marvellous creation that signifies both man's insignificance and his majesty at the same time, this awe-inspiring monument, a world heritage site, belongs indeed to all mankind.

It is not easy to imagine what might have passed through Kashyapa's mind, as he looked out of the palace window, at the far away moonlit skies. The last sighs of his father, mingled with the breeze that kissed the cool waters of Kalawewa, would have certainly disturbed him. Did he not repent the path he took to gain the crown of this island, which was but a mere speck against the myriad of stars in the infinite sky? Kashyapa's thoughts may have flown across towards the Kalawewa without ever being recorded on the Mirror Wall.

Nevertheless, the Sigiri Graffiti reflect the life force of Sinhala culture that reached its zenith in the Anuradhapura period.

The melodic verses of over seven hundred (later scholars have discovered several more) Sigiri poems, touched the chords of my heart, to resonate. Although I later embarked upon legal studies that (obviously) fell outside the realm of oriental literary and philosophic studies, my involvement with the Sigiri Graffiti never dwindled. Whenever I was overcome by loneliness, sadness or adversity, it was the Sigiri Graffiti that unfailingly came to my rescue like an ever obliging good friend.

Even after I accidentally drifted into politics, having resigned from my duties at the Legal Draftsman's Department my enchantment with the Sigiri Graffiti never left me but followed me constantly, enriching my outlook on life. Just as a precious gem, shines variously, depending on the angle of vision, so did the Sigiri Graffiti, in their pristine glory illumine my emotional world.

Indeed, how many times have I used the suppleness of Sigiri Graffiti in the academic world, on the political platform and in Parliamentary debate as the occasion demanded, just as an expert Ayurveda physician would use the same *Buddharaja kalka* as a therapy spiking it either with ginger, honey or lime juice to suit the needs of each ailment!

Poetry is a fount at which a *rasika* could quench his thirst according to his taste. It is a radiant star in the infinite sky. A star that radiates a soft light on a child gazing at it, sheds a light glowing with love on a forlorn lover staring at it. Just as the same star would provide a wise sage with the message of impermanence, poetry provides each individual with enrichment according to his age and taste.

I was fortunate to become the Minister of Cultural Affairs and Indigenous Medicine in the Cabinet of the late Hon. J.R.Jayewardene, who opened the door of politics for me and it was providential that I was able to complete the Dictionary started by Sir D.B.Jayatilaka, which at that time was moving at snail's pace, and present it to President Jayewardene himself. The post of the Leader of the House adorned by Sir Don Baron Jayatilaka was, in course of time, passed on to the representative of Haputale electorate in the Badulla district.

Many were the occasions when I, both in the government and in the opposition, tested the metaphor of the Sigiri verse which I used for the first time at that ceremonial rally in Haputale.

The Sigiri metaphor of the blind man on the lame man's shoulders came to my mind, when the Head of State came from one political party and the Prime Minister from another. Should one lament the lack of executive power and the other the lack of political clout? Should the two just idle on either side bemoaning their incapacity? Or should the lame one climb onto the shoulders of the blind one, so that both could move on? A start had to be made on an arduous journey with utmost patience and mutual co-operation.

Just as I spiked the Sigiri-verse, *Buddharaja* pellet with honey at the Diyatalawa village fair, I spiked it appropriately with lime juice in Parliament.

Addressing my friend the Attorney General, Late Mr. Kamalasabeyson PC and other attorneys-at-law headed by the Hon. Chief Justice, on my visit to the Attorney General's Department as the Minister of Justice to open its web site, I spiked the pellet not with honey or lime juice but with ginger. The manner in which judges mete out justice, weighing the evidence before them, ignoring what they personally saw or heard brought to my mind the image of the blindfolded Goddess of Justice.

Should not the lawyers headed by the Attorney General assist the judges to arrive at a just decision? But when they try to win victory for their own bigoted point of view, come what may, aren't they like lame men unable to move towards the truth? I interpreted the Sigiri metaphor of the blind man on the shoulders of the lame man to mean that although the Goddess of Justice with her eyes covered represented impartiality, the image also suggested that truth would remain inaccessible without the lawyers' co-operation. The Sigiri verse points out in no uncertain terms that truth may be accessed only with the mutual support of the judges and the lawyers.

The way our physicians use the *Buddharaja kalka* shows our own identity in adapting Ayurveda nurtured by Indian sages. Similarly, our identity suppressed by Sanskrit poetry over the centuries distinctly comes into its own in the wide range of the Sigiri verses.

Works such as *Elusandas Lakuna and Sidat Sangarava* clearly show that there had been a distinctive poetic tradition among us that went beyond the Indian poetry as revealed in the *Siyabaslakara*, Sinhala adaptation of the poetic treatise in Sanskrit named Kavyadarsha.Culminating this process *Kavsilumina,* the crest gem of the Sinhala poetic tradition, encases clearly the nuances and emotive expressions that are unique to the Sinhala tradition in both the everyday and the poetic worlds.

The Sigiri Graffiti adorn the Lion Rock as glowing examples of our own poetic tradition. It has sometimes been said of the Sigiri free verse that the poems lack elegance of rhythm. But free verse has organic rhythms of its own, generated by the logic of the experience and transcending formal structures.

To me, however, the Sigiri Graffiti means very much more. Besides being an endless source of personal enrichment, the vast range of attitudes, from adoration (eg. In Paranavitana's no. 381) to sensual arousal (no. 69), from emotional intensity (no. 249 ii) to sophisticated wit (no.320), and of expression, from the utmost directness (no. 278) to the cultured use of ***alamkara*** (no. 331), speak of the amazing richness of the culture of the Sinhala people in the heyday of the Anuradhapura period. As such, they are a challenge and an invitation to the ***rasikas*** and writers of today.

The mystique of Sigiriya lies in the splendours of its poetry. It is my fervent hope that this endeavour will contribute in some small way towards defining the importance of the poems and enhancing our appreciation of them.

W. J. M. Lokubandara

The Speaker's Residence,
Parliament Road,
Sri Jayewardhenepura Kotte,
Sri Lanka.

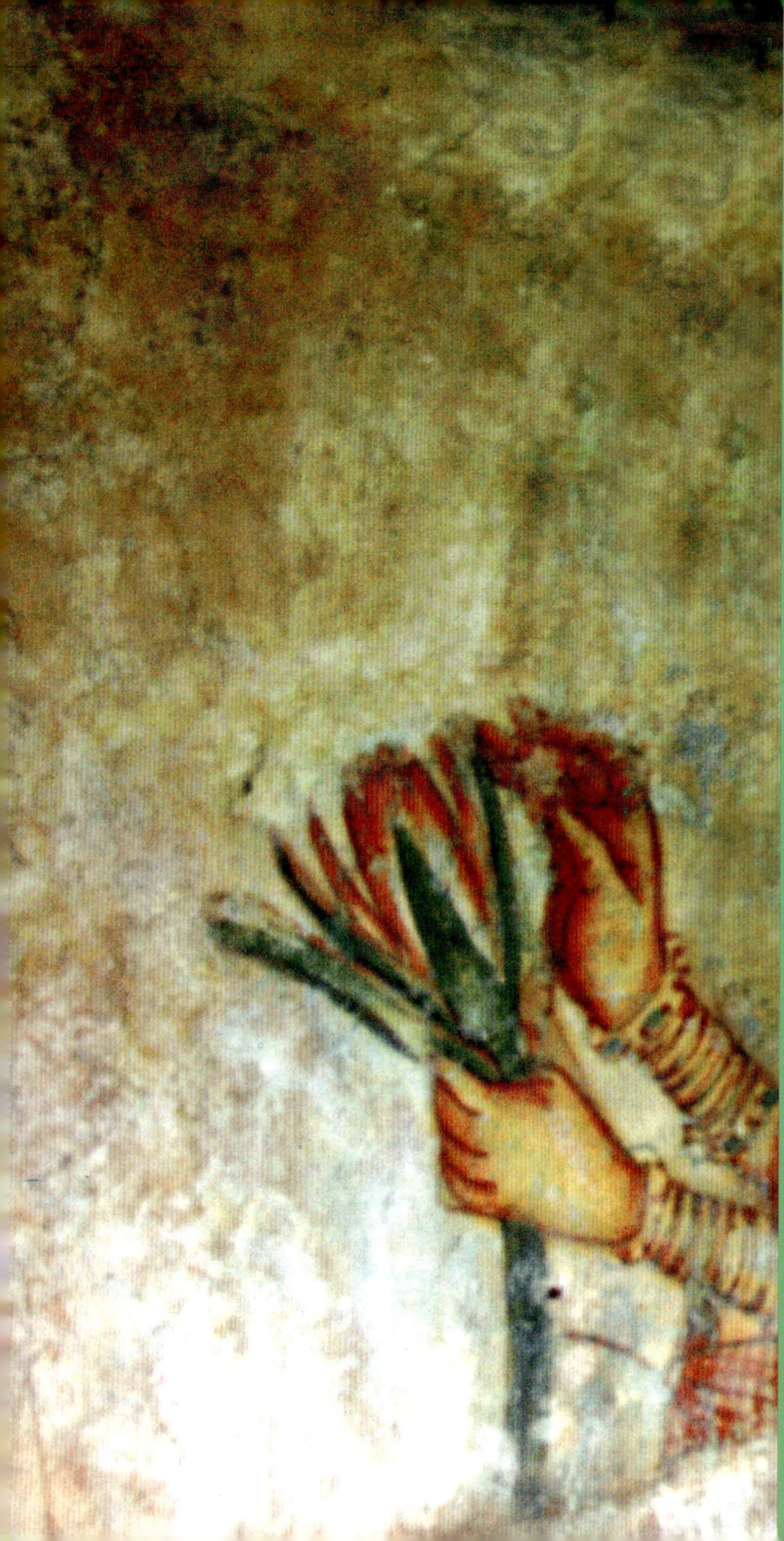

SIGIRI GEE SIRI - THE ENGLISH VERSION

In one of my frequent visits to Sri Lanka as Ambassador to UNESCO and France for duties associated with the UNESCO-SRI LANKA Cultural Triangle Project, **Honourable W.J.M. Lokubandara**, then the Minister of Cultural Affairs and now the Speaker of the Parliament, asked for my observations on his new book ***Sigiri Gee Siri***. Written in the most elegant *Sinhala* style, which is his own unique creation for effective communication in both speech and print, the book was so captivating that I read it overnight and had my comments for print by morning.

The charm of the book was twofold:

First, Wijamu – as we all call him with affection and esteem – has produced an extensive poem in prose of the Sigiri graffiti and brought each of the verses to life. This he has done with his remarkable talent for discovery and interpretation of the Indo–Sri Lankan tenets of critical literary appreciation or belles lettres;

Second, ever since Dr. Senerat Paranavitana, the painstaking epigraphist with a gift of imaginative creativity, had drawn the attention of the world literati to the wealth of literary masterpieces on the Mirror Wall of Sigiriya, my fascination for Sigiri verses had remained unabated. At first he did it through a talk to the Ceylon Branch of the Royal Asiatic Society (published in its Journal in 1940s and read by me in 1947 as a freshman in a Sinhala Class of Dr. P.E. Fernando, himself an epigraphist and literary critic). Wijamu's book satisfied a vital need – or even, in my case, an unquenchable thirst – to know more about these verses. The need existed for me to relive the ambience, in which many visitors from all ranks of society and from all areas of the Island gave expression to all kinds of deep emotions. These emotions were generated by the majestic rock and its environment and more so by the unparalleled beauties of the frescoes. How very cleverly Wijamu succeeded in this self-imposed venture is clearly evident.

The importance of translating Wijamu's work into English was immediately felt. Dr. Paranavitana's two volumes are scholarly studies written for the scholars with intricate details of every aspect of epigraphy, decipherment, interpretation, grammar and socio-historical background. His translations of verses concentrated on accuracy and fidelity to the original. His strict professional discipline hardly permitted him to digress in to flights of imaginative interpretation or search for alternative meanings or play with words. Wijamu's unique approach to literary appreciation not merely complements Dr. Paranavitana's work but adds an essential dimension of exploring with visionary overtones the psychological make-up of the poets, their thoughts and their strategies of expression. Wijamu's work, now available in English in this volume, is not only a companion volume to the erudite explorations of Dr. Paranavitana but also a veritable guide to enjoy at least three centuries of Sri Lankan literary creativity, represented solely by the graffiti.

Among Indo-Aryan languages of South Asia, Sinhala occupies an unparalleled position. It is the only language whose evolution is traceable from the early Prakrit form of the third or second century B.C.E. to its pulsating modern level of development – century by century through a treasure house of inscriptions that indicate the linguistic growth as well as the evolution of the script. Our literature whose extant works date back to over a thousand years, again, is a unique advantage. Nurtured by both Buddhist literature in Pali and Sanskrit as well as the ornate court poetry in Sanskrit, Sinhala Prakrit poetry dates back to a century before Christ. Poetry had dominated literary creativity and great poets whose works are no longer extant are recorded with esteem in literature.

The living proof to validate the antiquity of the poetic tradition of Sri Lanka comes from Sigiriya whose poetry pre-dates the earliest extant works. These verses, whose literary importance is amply highlighted by Wijamu in this book, also explain how and why the earliest extant work in Sinhala verse is a treatise on poetics – namely, *Siyabaslakara* – (literally, rhetorics of our own language). Broadly based on the Sanskrit work on poetics, Kāvyādavs's by Dandin (seventh century CE), this magnificent monograph of King Sena is an adaptation rather than a translation and its applicability to the prevailing Sinhala poetic norms is remarkable.

As Wijamu points out, the poets of Sigiriya were no mere charlatans but cultivated men of letters who were familiar with tenets of literary criticism and appreciation of the Indian subcontinent. The preponderance of such figures of speech as vakrokti, double entendre, anyālāpa, dhvani etc. receives special attention in Wijamu's meticulous analysis. He notes how dialogue (ubabas) figures as a typically Sinhala innovation with no parallel in Sanskrit. His sensitivity regarding semantic enhancement with just a simple syllable is illustrated with his in-depth discussion of the poetic values of an (any other) in the verse 26: balum mut ***an*** tepul no dun versus balum mut tepul no dum. (gave no ***other*** words but looks vs gave no words but looks). Reading these all too familiar sigiri verses with Wijamu's supersensitive insights is indeed a treat. Equally fascinating is his explanation of the special poetic form of the Sinhala language – the *Siyabasa* – for which alone *Sidatsangarawa* serves as a grammar.

I have been enthralled by two exposés by Professor Senake Bandaranayake and Dr. Roland Silva who showed me and my international UNESCO colleagues the rock wall facing the summer pavilion and called it the world's largest picture gallery. They told us that an area of at least one hundred meters by five meters was covered with frescoes to be seen and enjoyed from the pavilion. "Was it really so?" was a doubt we entertained at the time even though the theory appeared plausible. If only the information which Wijamu has in this book was then known to us. As the chapter entitled "The Five Hundred Damsels of Sigiriya" describes, how very convincing are the eye-witness accounts of Kit Sanboya in verse 44, Salabudu in verse 560 and Viravidur – Bata in verse 249 who actually saw in their time as many as five hundred damsels in the frescoes of this five-hundred-square meter picture gallery.

To Wijamu, every whim, fantasy or conjecture of the Sigiri graffiti–writers is a subject for research and penetrative analysis. The smile of damsels, their silence, the flowers in their hands etc. have evoked diverse reactions. Some fell in love at first sight and blamed the damsels for being unresponsive. Those who took the frescoes to be the ladies of King Kashyapa's harem moralized that they lacked decorum, for the damsels in frescoes were not in mourning for their dead consort. On the contrary, other poets saw the damsels as hurling down from the rock face in despair. Monks who philosophized on impermanence and royalty had their own views to express. Poets entered into literary arguments and even participated in contests. Some were more enthralled by the rock itself, the massive lion figure or just the lake. Among them was even Budal who came in company and refused to write a verse as all who came there wrote verses.

In analyzing the thought process of this wide range of writers, Wijamu lets his own investigation to take flights of incredible novelty. He looks for many meanings beside the obvious. In every instance, Wijamu searches for the poet's motive and motivation. Did flowers in hand have a special meaning? Were the flowers a symbol of love or even an overt invitation for intimacy? How and why did the smile of the damsels whose teeth resembled melon seeds bewitch some poets? Above all, the persisting question in the

Wijamu's mind has been the identity of the damsels. Who were they? He parades all theories so far expressed by archaeologists and art-historians and how each one has been ingenious in arriving at their conclusions. What Wijamu's search through Sigiri graffiti reveals is that visitors to the picture gallery down the ages had equally diverse identities for the damsels – ranging from divine or heavenly apsaras to women of the harem of King Kashyapa. What becomes patently clear is that the mystery will remain for ever unresolved and sky is the limit for speculation. It is a pity that a millennium has passed since the last poet wrote down his thoughts on the mirror wall!

Wijamu's analysis of the literary value of Sigiri verses anticipates a like-minded sympathy and aesthetic appreciation on the part of the reader. He expects the reader to be a sahṛda – a simple word but complex in meaning used in Sanskrit poetics. Meaning an aesthete or connoisseur, it literally could mean both "**having a heart**" in the sense of cultivated emotional responsiveness and "**sharing the heart or having a similar heart with the poet.**" Wijamu displays a capacity for both. His is a mature cultivated response to works of Sigiri poets and sees both their strengths and weaknesses. At the same time, he tries to get in to the heart – or, as we would say in common parlance, into the skin – of the poet. He becomes one with the poet and relives the latter's experience. He takes great pains to see the paintings and the environment with their eyes and, in this challenging endeavour, sees more than most of us would ever observe. To get the best of the special phenomenon of Wijamu's literary appreciation, the reader has to be patient, diligent and painstaking. Whenever one finds that Wijamu expresses the slightest enthusiasm, that passage should be read at least twice to get the best advantage. I have often read a passage even thrice over to immense profit.

My enjoyment of Wijamu's sensitive appreciation of the songs of Sigiriya has been redoubled by this English version. I commend that both the Sinhala original and the English version be read together or sequentially by those who can, because one does not replace the other. Until I had read both, I have not seen the incomparable literary value of the graffiti which thoughtful poets of the past have left to us as a lasting heritage. Thank you, Wijamu, for another laudable national service.

Ananda W. P. Guruge
Ph.D. (UC), D.Litt. (SJU), D.Litt. (RU)

Dean of Academic Affairs
University of the West, California, USA, and
Former Ambassador of Sri Lanka
to USA, France and UNESCO and
Senoir Special Advisor to the Director–General of UNESCO

THE SIGIRIYA POETRY AND THE AESTHETICS OF THE POPULAR POETIC TRADITION

Sigiri Gee Siri **written in 1990 by the well-known writer W.J.M.Lokubandara, created great enthusiasm in the Sinhala readership, about the culture of Sigiriya in general and Sigiri poetry in particular. With his "Sigiri Gee Siri" he was able to convey the essence of the poetical experimentation of the Sigiri poets who were inspired by all the aesthetically provocative aspects of Sigiriya.**

The present work is an English rendering of his "Sigiri Gee Siri"

Sigiriya is one of the main cultural sites of Sri Lanka, and is now considered as the eighth wonder of the world. It is a wonderful creation of human ingenuity on a site of awe-inspiring sublimity. It is a haven for classical Sinhalese art and architecture with its buildings, reservoirs, moats, walls, springs, and paintings. Although Sigiriya had a long history running from pre-historic times, its classical glory began in the 6th century by the efforts of King Kashyapa who established a citadel here. The entire construction was done during the brief period of his reign. The paintings on the rock surface consisted of female figures that added to the glory of Sigiriya. These female figures are delicately referred to as 'mahanel-vanun' (Blue-lily coloured) and 'ranvanun' (Golden-coloured) by the inspired visitors who wrote about them on the 'Mirror Wall.' Senerat Paranavitana, the eminent archaeologist discovered and fully deciphered verses numbering 685, written in the 8th, 9th and 10th centuries A.C. These verses that form an important part of

the cultural legacy is included in his two-volume work, the "Sigiri Graffiti" which is one of the most important, if not the most important contribution to Sri Lankan archaeology of the 20th century. Since the discovery of the verses by Paranavitana many more verses have been discovered on the 'Mirror Wall'.

While Lokubandara's Sinhala work, the "**Sigiri Gee Siri**", based on the above work, is extremely helpful for the Sinhala reader to understand the aesthetics of the graffiti, the present English rendering would serve in a complementary capacity to the two-volume *magnum opus* of Paranavitana, the "**Sigiri Graffiti**".

Paranavitana's primary concern in his work was that of an archaeologist, while that of Lokubandara is primarily that of an aesthete. His approach is that of a 'sahrda' who has developed a sort of symbiotic relationship with all that is at Sigiriya. As is mentioned in the Taittiriya Upanishad, the 'real' man passes from grosser forms to the subtler forms, through the physical, vital, mental, intellectual, culminating in the innermost beatific form. So, Lokubandara tries to glean the inner- most message/messages of the writers who wrote on the Mirror Wall. For the author it is a sort of re-discovery of his own beatific form, reached by careful observation, analysis and enjoyment, and it is this that he invites the reader to share with him in this work. Like the 'real' man who passes through the five stages, the author, in all seriousness, tries to guide the reader to the 'nectar of song', as he himself puts it. However, it must be emphasized that his aesthetic considerations are thoroughly based on a keen scholar-critic's stance. It is in this sense that it serves in a complementary capacity to the Sigiri Graffiti of Paranavitana.

The salient feature of Lokubandara's effort is that he intends his work to be a key to introduce the reader to Paranavitana's masterpiece through the avenue of aesthetic enjoyment the intended purpose of the Sigiri poets. In his work he rarely disagrees with the original work of Paranavitana: he builds on it; makes it more meaningful; re-arranges the material thematically so that the reader may have an in-depth notion of what is highlighted by the writers of the graffiti. Thus it may not be out of place here if we consider a few high points of Paranavitana's "Sigiri Graffiti" itself so that the importance of Lokubandara's work could be better appreciated.

The "Sigiri Graffiti" is a masterly archaeological contribution, a work that cannot easily be superseded. In this work, Paranavitana delves into all imaginable aspects of the graffiti including higher textual criticism, going much beyond what is simply of archaeological importance. Aspects such as, the nature of the documents and their decipherment, orthography, palaeography, grammar, language of the graffiti, prosody, the literary quality of the documents, the subject matter of the documents, and the authors are all carefully studied in atomistic detail. There is nothing left for speculation and conjecture. In dealing with most of these aspects he traces their development up to the time of Sigiriya and connects them with the subsequent developments wherever necessary. The sections on orthography, palaeography, grammar and prosody are so detailed that they could be regarded as independent works on their own. (M.H.Peter Silva translated into Sinhala the section on grammar under the title Sigiri-gi-viyaranaya). In his treatment of the literary quality of the documents, relevant for our purpose here, he masterfully uses the traces of literary criticism found in the graffiti, along with celebrated notions of both Indian and Western theories of aesthetics and art criticism in his valuation of Sigiri poems. This, I think, is the first time that Practical Criticism came to be seriously applied to judge any Sinhala literary work. The graffiti won the highest admiration of Paranavitana as poetry of a high order on thematic, stylistic as well as aesthetic grounds.

The discovery of the Sigiri poems is of utmost importance to Sinhala culture. They were discovered at a time when the colonial impact was still felt and even the classical literature was not properly appreciated. The entire classical literary tradition was disparagingly considered as a mere religious tradition confined mainly to translations from Pali sources. There was a break in the cultural tradition after about the 10th century that gave way to slavish imitation of Sanskrit models. This degeneration continued during the subsequent times so that there was a vast gap between the cultural achievements of this early period and the later times. In fact, Robert Knox who wrote in the 17th century about these classical works could not imagine that they were by 'Chingulays' (Sinhalese people).

"The Pagodas or Temples of their Gods are so many that I cannot number them. Many of them are rare and exquisite work, built of hewn stone, engraven with images and figures; but by whom and when I could not claim to know, the inhabitants themselves being ignorant therein. But sure I am they were built by far more ingenious Artificers, than the Chingulays that are on the land. For the Portuguese in their invasions have defaced some of them, which there is none found that hath skill enough to repair to this day". (Historical Relations of Ceylon, Pp 115-116).

It was later confirmed that all these exquisite works were by the Sinhalese and no others. However, that the poems which we deal with here are definitely by Sinhala writers is confirmed by the fact that they were written in Sinhala, or Hela as Lokubandara wishes to refer to it. Simhala>Sihala>Hela simply is the language of the Sinhalese. But the epithet Hela or Elu is generally used to refer to the 'pure form' of the language that the ancient Sinhalese developed and preserved as their 'poetical' language as well as the language of national identity. It is clear from this distinctive

Hela form of language that although languages such as Sanskrit and Pali had a great bearing on the culture of the Sinhalese throughout, the Sinhalese, who were conscious of their self-identity, persistently held on to the Hela language, in the same way they cling to Buddhism – their national faith. For Lokubandara, the fact that the graffiti are in the Hela language is itself an important consideration for his endeavour. He is keenly aware of the endeavours of Kumaratunga (1887-1944) who made a sustained effort to resuscitate the Hela style of writing in the 20th century. For Kumaratunga, Hela meant not only the use of pure Sinhala words but also correct grammar, brevity, logicality and economy in language use as exemplified in the best of classical writings. The graffiti here shows the earliest instance of the use of Hela language in poetry, and Kumaratunga's high estimate of it is confirmed by the achievements of the Sigiri poets. It is unfortunate that Kumaratunga himself did not live long enough to see his convictions about the genius of Hela language being confirmed by the discovery of the graffiti that represent the earliest and the best specimens of it. It is well known that Lokubandara himself is one of the foremost exponents of the Hela movement, and it is justifiable that he takes great interest in the graffiti. Thus, we should be keenly aware that Sigiri poems not only display the talents of the poets of the times but also the ingenuity of the Hela language. Here we are dealing with a language of poetry that nearly all Sigiri poets share as their medium of poetical thought. This Hela form of language continued during subsequent times too as the esteemed form of poetical expression, well up to modern times. Prose drew on the colloquial as well as the highbrow Sanskrit lexical and stylistic deviations, but for poetry Hela reigns supreme even now. It is true that some who wish to make radical changes try to deviate from it, but such attempts have ended up in failure for the reason that products based on such deviations cannot match the elegance of the earlier poetical tradition enshrined in the Hela form of the language. So there is a great enthusiasm on the part of the author Lokubandara to not only find the aesthetics of the poems concerned, but also to foreground the genius of the Hela language which is associated closely with the native aesthetics of the Sinhalese. This impact of Hela form is so pervasive that even after so many centuries the innermost emotions of the Sinhalese could be stirred by it. Even the single classical grammar of the language, the *Sidath Sangarava* (13th century) makes an attempt to provide grammatical rules intended to sustain this all too important literary form of language which by that time has been challenged by what is called the exegetical style (Arutviyakana), used in prose translations from Sanskrit to Pali sources. This hybrid prose style made inroads on pure Sinhala (Hela) prose after about the 12th century. The *Sidath Sangarava* introduces such prosaic arut-viyakana usages as deviations rather than approved core grammatical features. From the standpoint of this grammar, the *sine qua non* of amateur poets should be the mastery of grammatical as well as poetical usages of the Hela language that the author proudly refers to as the Siyabasa or Native Language. It must also be mentioned that Kumaratunga, in the same manner as the author of the *Sidath Sangarava* was highly critical of the arut-viyakana style as a phenomenon that sapped away the genius of the Sinhala language. The reason is that this exegetical mould of language introduced unnecessary expository or exegetical trappings and too much verbiage.

We have made it clear that Lokubandara's main objective for the present endeavour is the introduction of the reader to the aesthetics of Sigiri verses. However, this is only an overt estimate of his work. If one were to probe further, it is apparent that his real preoccupation is with the Hela language whose genius is enshrined in many of the poems found here. Written by over at least 600 poets/versifiers, the message/messages, though important in themselves, take a back seat as it were, while the medium, the Hela language, in all its elegance is highlighted. As could be expected, all those who wrote here were not poets; what was common to all of them was the language. In general, the writings belonging to three successive centuries display some internal development, but yet dialectic deviations are difficult to come by, although the poets themselves hailed from all parts of the country. Therefore, it seems that poetic language had by this time evolved a standard form to be readily used by the poets. People from many different regions visited Sigiriya (Paranavitana lists about 125 places) and they, as mentioned earlier, belong to different strata of society, but strangely enough we do not find much regional or social deviations in the language. It points to the fact that the language had become standardized even at that early stage. It was a common heritage of the writers so that who ever wished to write verses could do so. Moreover, even the writers who came out with the simplest of poetic expression were adept in their use of language. For example, the following poem that many would not rate as a poem displays great ability on the part of the writer in his use of language with its metrical composition, rhyme and, more importantly, the rhythm and musicality that emphasize the intended lyrical quality of an Ode to Sigiriya:

Si raju yasasa siri
Tubu mulu lov patiri
Nilupulasun asiri
Balumo Sihigiri (205)

'We saw at Sihigiri the king of lions, whose fame and splendour remain spread in the whole world, and the wonderful damsels with eyes (like) blue lilies.'

These poems in the Hela language are credited with many FIRSTS, which should also be borne in mind when dealing with them. They are the

FIRST specimens of poetry in the New Indo Aryan language called **Hela** that emerged from the Sinhala Prakrit during the sixth or seventh century A.C. In fact, they are to be reckoned as the FIRST writings of any of the New Indo Aryan Languages. In this connection it should be noted that Sinhala evolved much faster than the N.I.A. languages of India which came into existence only after the 10th century and whose literary experiments are later than 12th century A.C. Written during the creative stage of Sinhala culture, they are the FIRST secular writings before religious themes based on Pali sources became the main stay of the classical literature. The literature that emerged after about the 10th century is IMITATIVE rather than CREATIVE to a large extent. Thematically the poets of the classical times were obliged to keep to religious themes and adhere stylistically to the emerging Sanskrit norms that influenced all literatures of South and South East Asia, especially during the time of the Hindu kingdoms of the region whose lingua franca was Sanskrit. It may be said that the Sigiri poets were consciously using the **Hela** language. They were keenly aware of its capacity to evoke the aesthetic emotions of the Sinhala readers. The imitative language of the later times, found in Gee poems was meant for only those who were conversant with and appreciated the Sanskrit poetical embellishments both in meaning and sound. In contrast, as all and sundry have tried their hand at writing poetry in Sigiriya, we can safely say that the graffiti are representative of the 'popular poetic tradition' of the times. Further, this popular tradition had all the ingredients of 'high motivation' and 'high aesthetic' sensibility.

One of the main features that Paranavitana emphasizes is that the poets were keenly aware of the cultural norms of the society and never succumbed to vulgarity, although the subject matter of women in the paintings presented such an opportunity. Even the slightest vulgarity was denounced in no uncertain terms as when a poet who criticized those who only wrote about the eyes of women and not of their breasts was referred to as a 'haughty boor' (mindibi gahaviya). That writing of poetry was not restricted to only the learned, but to any one who had the inclination to do so is clearly affirmed by the poetry here. It is indeed an instance where the kings, ministers, clergy, women of different social status, ordinary citizens as well as poets who came from various parts of the country were provided with an equal opportunity to try their hand at poetry.The variety of their thoughts, borne out of their individual situations in life, show the creativity of a nascent literature that was a 'common pursuit' and a 'communal enterprise' rather than something restricted to only the sophisticated and the learned. It is the FIRST time we can identify something that could be called 'people's literature' well before such literature came into being with Socialism. There is of course a difference in that, while the former refers to literature 'by' the people while the latter refers to literature 'for' the people.

Another is the fact that it is the FIRST time that poetry of such an ancient period is presented and preserved as the very autographs of the writers. Apart from the natural damages, the poems are intact as poetic expressions, so that they could be utilized as parameters to judge the mental culture of the times. In fact, it is in this aspect that Lokubandara is most interested.

Lokubandara's contribution to Sigiriya is not confined to this work alone. The Sigiri Graffiti, first published in 1956 by the Oxford University Press was reprinted in 1982 for wider circulation on his initiative. At that time, he also had an idea of getting this work translated into Sinhala with its long introduction forming its first volume. Nandasena Mudiyanse has translated the graffiti into Sinhala, leaving out most of the notes and comments found in the original. K. Jayatilake has also edited and translated the poems, sometimes giving different interpretations, but never deviating too much from Paranavitana's original.

Inspired by the setting, paintings and the graffiti, well known Irish poet Richard Murphy wrote 61 poetical pieces titled "The Mirror Wall". These poems, though inspired by the graffiti, are creations of the author, mainly intended for the present day reader.

I do not wish to go into details of the poetical quality of the poems. They are brief, lyrical, and more interestingly are some of the best experiments in the Hela language. This poem by a Buddhist novice, probably a teenager, shows his skill in writing poetry:

Vesey jana e ki savanihi rakaneya sihi la
Mana maya biyi kara ha pulahasu vijanina tatanuya (No. 88)

"The person spoken about is here;
'Place mindfulness in the ear and protect it'!
I am agitated by her broad smile
And my mind trembles exceedingly'

The above reaction by a novice upon seeing a beautiful woman is personal and opens a wide field of semantics. He has come here with a prior knowledge of the female figure referred to in the poem. Upon seeing her he advises himself to be alert and protect the mind. The monks are to be mindful of what they see, hear, smell, taste, contact and think, eye, ear, nose, tongue, body and mind being the doors through which lust or desires can infect a person. The monk here has already been ensnared by seeing the woman so that he is not in a position to protect his eye. That is why ear in the order of sequence comes to his mind almost habitually. However, by now his mind itself has been assailed by the beauty of the woman. Alas, there is no escape for him despite his religious training! Though overtly he tries to regain his composure, the suggestion is that at least temporarily he could not resist the temptation of the woman in the painting. One may also see some irony in the expression.

The introduction and notes and observations of the author Lokubandara are immensely helpful to understand what Sigiriya signifies. He arranges the subject matter of Sigiri poems under twelve sections, using some of the favourite expressions of the poets themselves. Under each of the headings he has given the original and translations of some of the best poems so that the reader will get a glimpse of the glorious culture of the classical times. The author sometimes uses the renderings by Paranavitana, but often makes his own poetical trans-creations or adaptations. When it comes to interpretation of poetical expressions, the author takes the general theme into consideration. Where he deviates from the matrix, his creations become an admixture of both the matrix and target codes and evolve a distinctive semantic code. Thus Lokubandara's translations are trans-creations, meriting the attention of critics and translators. In such radical translations he displays his own poetic talents.

Sigiriya is located in the Inamaluwa Korale of the Matale District. Sigiriya is one of the main cultural sites of Sri Lanka, and is now considered as the eighth wonder of the world. It is a wonderful creation. It is a haven for classical Sinhalese art and architecture with its buildings, reservoirs, moats, walls, springs, and paintings. Although Sigiriya had a long history running from pre-historic times, its classical glory began in the 6th century by the efforts of King Kashyapa who established a Palace here. The entire construction was done during the brief period of his reign. The paintings on the rock surface consisted of female figures that added to the glory of Sigiriya. Since the discovery of the verses by Professor Paranavitana many more verses have been discovered on the 'Mirror Wall'.

The discovery of the Sigiri poems is of utmost importance to Sinhala culture. They were discovered at a time when the colonial impact was still felt and even the classical literature was not properly appreciated. The Lion figure, ponds, forest parks are incomparable creations of the time.

Getting back to the literary ethos of Lokubandara's work, it is apt to repeat that the introduction, notes and observations made by him reveal all what Sigiriya signifies.

Prof. P. B. Meegaskumbura

ENFRAMING SIGIRI POETRY

The Sigiri graffiti constitute a very rich and important segment of classical Sinhala poetry. Written largely during the period from the 8th to the 10th centuries, although some of the verses belong to an earlier period, this body of poetry is marked by a compression of form, wit, playfulness, an acute drama of argument, and an imagination of a high order. The strength of these poems is to be seen in the way in which they work within the rubrics of inherited rhetorical frameworks. Many of the poems are responses, some spontaneous, some studied, to the beautiful figures drawn on the Sigiriya wall. The flawed innocence of the damsels depicted in the paintings, as refracted through the imagination of the Sigiri poets, makes for lyrically intense and dramatically poignant poetry. Many of these poems are highly compact, where silences, suppressions of feeling and half-articulated thoughts play a crucial role in poetic communication. For that very reason, forms of deconstructive reading, the Derridean type as well as the line of enquiry stretching from Bhartrihari's the Vakyapadiya to Anadavardhana's Dhvanyaloka can be invoked very productively. These paintings, the poetry and the fortress of Sigiriya (Lion Mount) in general signify a cultural experience of very great importance. The rock of Sigiriya, which is about 200 metres in height, rises above the surrounded jungle flanked by the gardens and the lake. King Kashyapa (477 – 485 A.D.), established his capital here, having murdered his father and chased away his half-brother. It is in order to overcome these unpleasant emotions that he constructed the aesthetically marvellous complex that is Sigiriya and this along with the scopophilia displayed in the paintings and poetry would make the Sigiriya experience a marvellous site for Freudian analyses.

Mr. W.J.M.Lokubandara has produced an exposition of some of the Sigiri poems and sought to place them in their proper historical, linguistic and cultural context. He treats them as cultural texts that yield up their riches with each careful and imaginative hermeneutical exegesis. The richness of the Sigiri graffiti was uncovered by Senerat Paranavitana over a period of three decades. His was a monumental effort that won the gratitude of the nation. Subsequent scholars expanded on, supplemented, challenged and subverted some of the ideas of Paranavitana. But whatever the disagreements among scholars regarding details and points of interpretation, it is evident that Paranavitana's effort constituted an inescapable reference point.

Mr. Lokubandara's attempt is to display the literary power and complexity inscribed in these verses. Many of the writings on Sigiri graffiti deal with the linguistic, historical and scholarly dimensions: Lokubandara, while not ignoring this aspect of Sigiri graffiti, has sought to focus on the literary and aesthetic dimensions. The outcome is a book that should prove to be of great value to the educated lay English reader. His comments, pithy, relevant and always insightful, serve to widen the horizon of understanding of the English reader. Let us for example consider the way he alludes to the cultural topoi embedded in Sigiri poetry. The concept of topos, which figured so prominently in classical rhetoric and dialectic, has resurfaced in modern literary studies as an important instrument of analysis. Topos is a Greek word that designates the idea of place and is generally used to denote a commonplace that had a direct bearing on the structure and conventions pertaining to a given work of literature in Aristotelian rhetoric; a topos served to generate new ideas; it alluded to the places in one's mind that one goes to find arguments. It helps one to frame an issue and bring a distinctive perspective to it; hence topos is an analytical instrument that can be extremely useful in imposing an order on one's experience, ruminations, and thoughts and in establishing a shared world of perception. Clearly, it figures prominently in literary communication.

The relation between topoi and a given culture is an intimate one, in that topoi both reflect and intervene in the deeper structures of culture. The topoi found in the classical Chinese literary tradition are different from those found in classical Sanskrit tradition, and they, taken together, display a remarkable divergence from the topoi of European traditions. These disparities and dissimilarities can be largely explained by means of culture. In any culture, literary topoi arise in certain periods, undergo transformation as they engage with other created traditions, disappearing and resurfacing. Studying topoi and the historical relations and specificities with which they are connected can offer us much useful information regarding the epistemes that held sway in different periods in culture. Topoi serve to order and frame discussions; they also put into play fixity and movement, history and contemporaneity, antiquity and newness, authority and freedom. A careful analysis of a work like the Sahityadarpana would surely demonstrate the organizing power of topoi in literary textuality.

The complex use of topoi can be seen in the classical Indian tradition, as indeed in many other classical Asian traditions where it helped to usher in a greater depth of exploration into creativity. For example, the topos of renunciation, which is pivotal to most Indian traditional thought, has generated a body of exquisite poetry of human complexities and uncertain play of desire – a poetry that both mediates on and enacts the power of human desire. Renunciation was deemed a supreme objective leading to deeper insights into human existence and ultimately to liberation from the endless cycle of births and deaths. Hindu and Buddhist literature contains graphic exemplifications of this. For example, in the Buddhist Theri Gatha (verses of the nuns), the central topos is that of the joys of renunciation. However, the way in which this topos was worked out in the poems brought into play tensions and contradictions between the mundane and the supramundane, the material and the spiritual, serving to enhance the power of the poetry. For example, in one of the poems, a nun sees her body as, 'an old house with its plaster fallen off,' and reveling in the ecstasies of renunciation, recaptures her past. In doing so, she summons up powerful worldly and sensuous images that contrast sharply with her present tranquility.

My hair was black
Like the hive of bees
With curly ends.
With fine pins
Decked out with gold
Beautiful with plaits
My hair looked enticing.

My eyes shone
Resplendent like jewels
Dark blue and long.

Here, the contraries between the worldly and the other-worldly, sensuous and spiritual, invest these poems with a human complexity one would not normally expect from a work celebrating the renunciation of household life. I have chosen to dwell at length on the notion of topos, because it is vital to appreciating the true strength of Sigiri poetry. The central topos animating many of the poems on the Sigiri Wall is that of appearance and its problematic ontology. The interplay between the paintings and poetry, the visual and literary objects, feeds into this topos. The self-confrontation that results in displaying the unreality of the reality encountered is given sharper focus in these poems through the topos of appearance. As one poet says, 'they give no other speech but glances from their motionless eyes'; this captures this nature of the topos I am alluding to very effectively. There is a three-fold dialogue coursing through these poems: a dialogue with the paintings, a dialogue with earlier respondents, and a dialogue with the poet himself or herself. This three-fold dialogue serves to underline the animating power of the topos that I referred to earlier.

Topoi can be used imaginatively to uncover both broader cultural bonds. A recent example of this being Henryk Markiewicz's commentary on the topos, 'as is painting so is poetry' in New Literary history 18:3, 1987. This has a pointed relevance to the poetry of Sigiriya. Here the identification of poetry and painting as well as the reflections of differences in qualities and values are examined from a historical perspective, thereby opening an interesting window onto Western cultural thinking.

It seems to me that beyond the introduction of these poems as significant cultural texts, Mr. Lokubandara has focused on two intersecting issues of great importance to cultural critics and literary scholars. The first is the issue of literary history. Literary history and philology used to occupy a very prominent place in literary study; today, as George Watson points out, we are witnessing the 'sharp descent of literary history from the status of a great discipline.' [1]. Rene Wellek bemoans the fall of literary history.[2]

The developments in literary theory during the last fifty years or so have contributed much to the dislodgement of literary history from its clear position of eminence. The new critics, with their emphasis on the work of literature as a verbal icon, paid scant attention to the question or origin, of social and cultural background. Structuralists – with their preoccupation with synchrony, as opposed to diachronic and the issue of literariness and how a literary text actually works, as opposed to questions of genesis, value etc. - ignored the historical imagination. Northrop Frye, with his formidable explorations into archetypes and a universal and timeless order of literature, severely undermined the efficacy of historical studies in literature and in more recent times, the writings of post-structuralists like Jacques Derrida, Roland Barthes, Paul de Man, J. Hillis Miller, with their decidedly Ahistorical stance, their stress on the absence of origin, structure, and their emphasis on the free play of signifiers tended to further emasculate literary history as a serious academic discipline. Paul de Man has made the following revealing observation.

"We are concerned at this point with the question of whether the history of an entity as self-contradictory as literature is conceivable. In the present state of literary study this possibility is far from being clearly established. It is generally admitted that a positivistic history of literature, treating as it were a collection of empirical data, can only be a history of what literature is not. At best, it would be a preliminary classification opening the way for actual literary study, and at worst, an obstacle in the way of literary understanding."[3]

The question of reference looms very large in the post-structuralists agenda of literary study. They believe that literary texts are self-enclosed verbal texts which have no relation to a reality outside and prior to the text. Hillis Miller talks of the 'fiction of the referential'[4], which Umberto Eco alludes to the 'referential fallacy'[5]. Derrida flatly denies that there is anything outside the text[6]. Paul de Man, who has been the most powerful voice representative of this anti-referential post-structuralist approach says, that the reference is the non-verbal outside of which language refers, by which it is constituted and upon which it acts[7]. De Man's point seems to be that there is no domain outside the text because of our inability as readers to identify such a domain with any degree of certainty from the text. He feels that the disjunction between text and external reality rests on an inside/outside metaphor that has not been seriously challenged. Roland Barthes asserted that all writing is narcissistic activity and that reality is only a pretext; that writing cannot explain the world.[8] Northrop Frye remarked that literary texts do not enter into a referential relationship with the world in the way those sentences of daily speech do, and that literary texts are not representative of anything but themselves[9].

This approach to referentiality and texts, not surprisingly, has been challenged by many perceptive scholars. As Jerome McGann has remarked, what is needed is not to bracket the referential dimensions of literature out of critical consideration on the basis of an impoverished theory of language and literary reference but to try and recover and reformulate the idea of referentiality which underlies the thought of the distinguished historical critics of the recent past. As he points out, to recover the concept of referentiality, we need to be aware that facts are not mere objects of data, but are heuristic isolates that bring to the fore a nexus of events, relations, and processes.[10] Similarly Weimann expresses the view that post-structuralist's view of the absence of referentiality and the hegemony of discourse implies the rise and decline of representation which pays inadequate attention to gaps and links between, what is representing and what is represented.[11] it is precisely in these gaps and links that historical and referential activity can be said to take place. Clearly, Mr. W.J.M.Lokubandara sides with the second group of theorists. He realizes the significance of referentiality and historicity in textual production, but does not articulate it in a high-handed fashion. What better venue to press the arguments related to referentiality and historicity of poetry than the writings in Sigiriya?

As one examines Lokubandara's examination of the Sigiri poetry as cultural texts one is made aware of the fact that contextualization and re-contextualization, according to Lokubandara, marks an important aspect of critical exegesis. The concept of context is as important as that of reference in any discussion of literary history. There is a danger in assuming the context to be monolithic and uncomplex, thereby underestimating the subtleties involved in literary historical investigations. As LaCapra points out, in seeking to return a writer to his or her time, there is a real danger of simplifying the process of historical understanding, the rhetoric of contextualization has prompted documentary readings in which the text becomes little more than the sign of the time.[12] Hayden White says that it is not unusual for literary theorists, when they are discussing the context of a literary work, to assume that this context or historical milieu has a specific accessibility that the work itself can never have.[13] So it is important to pay attention to the complex dynamics associated with the context. There is a need to reject both the simplistic and simplifying traditional view of literary history which posits a clear cut context and the post-structuralist view which sees the text as self-enclosed and self-negating entity. It is to the credit of Lokubandara that he has avoided both extremes in his valorization of history and context of Sigiri poetry.

The second important and related issue that Lokubandara focuses on in his critical commentaries on Sigiri poetry is the way in which we should evaluate and assess classical works. Broadly speaking, there are two methods of approach to ancient literary works. The first is to situate them strictly in their historical period of origin and treat them as period-pieces. Consequently, the only way in which they can emerge into the present is as museum-pieces; there is no attempt here to probe into the contemporary relevance of these texts, and how they could contact with modern structures of feeling. This is, in a way, a forced imprisonment within history. The second approach is to treat them as pieces of contemporary writing with no reference to the specificities of their historical and cultural background and use modern concepts and tools of evaluation as if these are works of twenty-first century authors. Both methods of approach are defective, and should be avoided. This is exactly what Lokubandara does in examining Sigiri poetry as supremely important cultural texts. He is fully alive to the complex ways in which history and the imperatives of the time have inflected the content, form, and strategies of representation of these poems. On the other hand, he has no desire to shackle them to their periods of origin. He is keen to explore the contemporary cultural pulse contained in them by subjecting them to the hermeneutical exegesis; the Gadamerian fusion of horizons is clearly discernible in his perceptive commentaries.

All in all, Mr.W.J.M.Lokubandara's translations of Sigiri poetry, and his critical comments on them, display the focused scholarship, literary sensitivity and poetic imagination that one has come to associate with the writer. He is passionately moved by the controlled lyricism of Sigiri poetry, and he wishes to share that joy with a wider circle of connoisseurs. That proclivity clearly shines through in his translations as well as his critical comments. Lokubandara, by publishing this work, has performed a most useful service in cultural ambassadorship. He is Speaker of Parliament of

Sri Lanka. Constitutionally speaking, he is the third most powerful person in the country next to the President and Prime Minister. That a politically important and a busy person such as Lokubandara could find the time to produce a work of this nature is indeed astonishing. What is even more astonishing is the scholarship, cultural sensitivity and the apprehension of problems of hermeneutic exegeses that he displays; it is most impressive. What other Speaker of the World has published a scholarly and imaginative work of this significance?

References

1. George Watson, The Study of Literature (London: Allen Lane. The Penguin Press, 1969) 66
2. Rene Wellek, The Attack on Literature (Chapel Hill: Unviersity of North Carolina Press, 1982) 64-72
3. Paul de Man, Blindness and Insight: Essays on the Rhetoric of Contemporary Criticism (Minneapolis: University of Minnesota Press, 1983) 162
4. J. Hillis Miller, Stevens Rock and Criticism as Cure, Georgia review 30 (1976) 29
5. Umberto Eco. A Theory of Semiotics (Bloomington: Indiana University Press, 1976)
6. Jacques Derrida, Of Grammatology (Baltimore: Johns Hopkins University Press, 1976)
7. Paul de Man, 164
8. Roland Barthes, Essais Critiques (Paris; Seruil, 1964)
9. Northrop Frye, Anatomy of Criticism (New York; Anthenum Press, 1966)
10. Jerome J. McGann, ed. Historical Studies and Literary Criticism (Madison; University of Wisconsin Press, 1985) 7
11. Robert Weimann, History, Appropriation and the Uses of Representation in Modern Narrative in The Aim of Representation ed. M. Krieger (New York; Columbia Univeristy Press, 1987) 176
12. Dominick LaCapra, Rethinking Intellectual History: Texts, Contexts, Language (Ithaca: Cornell University Press, 1983) 14
13. Hayden White, Tropics of Discourse (Baltimore: Johns Hopkins University Press, 1978) 65

Prof. Wimal Dissanayake

Director,
East-West Centre,
Academy for Creative Media,
University of Hawaii

SIGIRI GĪ
THE MIRROR WALL POEMS

It is not often recognized that some of the most astonishing documents in the ancient world are the Sigiri graffiti. Consisting of more than 1500 surviving writings, many of them fragmentary, they are in a true sense unique, with no parallel elsewhere. Nearly 700 graffiti were read and published by Senarat Paranavitana in the 1950s and another 820 deciphered more recently by Benille Priyanka. They record the individual thoughts, feelings and emotions of hundreds of visitors to the remains at the historic palace site of Sigiriya – a World Heritage city – over a time span of nearly eight hundred years, from the beginning of the sixth century onwards.

The greater part of the Sigiri graffiti dates from the eighth to the tenth centuries and is in verse. These verses, which form the subject of the present book, are mostly poems addressed to the female figures depicted on the rock face above the Mirror Wall, a highly polished protective wall forming part of the ascent to the palace on the summit of the precipitous Sigiriya rock. They are in essence poems about paintings, 'art about art'.

In W J M Lokubandara's *Sigiri Gī The Mirror Wall Poems* we have the first book length literary appraisal in English of the poems contained in the Sigiri graffiti. The very title of the original Sinhala edition of the present book, *Sigiri Gī Siri*, beautifully captures the classic elegance and refinement of the Sigiriya poems, which occupy a distinctive place – literary, contextual and historical – in a widespread Asian tradition of epigrammatic poetry.

The English version of *Sigiri Gī Siri,* like the original publication, analyses the poetry with keen insight and sensitivity and introduces this modern reading of the Sigiriya verses to an international audience. It invites the attention of a wider range of readers, writers and scholars than those who have hitherto had access to the Sigiriya poems.

Prof. Senake Bandaranayake

ACKNOWLEDGEMENT

Down the few years when the idea of writing this book was conceived within me, the number who collaborated with me in this work have been so many as to defy enumeration. There is a popular line etched on our *Katarama* or drip-ledges that donates the rocky enclaves to our revered monks as habitats.

"Agata anagata catu – disa – sagasa"

(This cave is gifted) to the Sangha of the four quarters, present and absent"

I will take the liberty of transforming this hallowed and famous line of our monastic history "to thank those who helped in my work in large measure and in all sorts of minor ways too."

Please bear with me if a particular name has been left out for the omission is not deliberate. Their names will remain etched forever in my heart for treating this work as their own and performing whatever I asked them to do for me to put out a successful literary production.

My Guru Mr. D. D. Dias, Dr. Ananda Guruge, Prof. Wimal Dissanayaka, Prof. P. B. Meegaskumbura, Prof. Senake Bandaranayaka, Prof. Ashley Halpé, Dr. Patrick Ratnayake, Prof. Lakshmi De Silva, Dr.Tissa Abeysekera, Dr. D. B. Nihalsingha, Dr. Siri Gunasighe, Mrs. Padma Edirisinghe, Mrs. Eileen Siriwardena, Prof. A. V. Suraveera, Prof. Vini Vitharana, Mr. Sandadas Coperahewa, Mr. Upul Jayantha Ranepura, Mr. Edmund Jayasuriya, Mr. Harold Peiris, Ms. Vishva Karunaratne, Mr. Sarath Samarasekera, Mr. Mahinda Guneratna, Mr. P. Hewage and at last, but not least my three sons - Rashmin, Udith & Damith have contributed their share in various ways. And of course Mr. Sirisumana Godage (Proprietor of Godage International) and Mr. Narada Karunatilaka, Ms.Ganga Kumudini, Priyangika Kothalawala, Thanoja Priyadarshani and Hiranthi Lanka of the same staff earn my thanks.

W. J. M. Lokubandara

MAY THEIR IDENTITY REMAIN UNSOLVED FOR EVER!

The lithic inscription, discovered in 1964, in the vicinity of Timbiri Wewa (Reservoir) at Maradanmaduwa, in Wilpattu, identifies Kasyapa I with "Kasabala Alakapaya" or "Kasyapa Alakapati" (Kasyapa the Lord of Mount Alaka). According to the *Mahavamsa* King Kasyapa built atop The Lion Rock "a comely palace resembling the second Ālakamandā and lived there like Kuvera". 14 (1) *Mahavamsa* – Chap. 39.

Extending this concept further afield, Senarat Paranavitana asserts that the ladies depicted in the Sigiri frescoes are an integral part of the Alakapura idea which is the theme of his work "The Story of Sigiri". It seems appropriate to summarize here the references in this work to the events which led to the construction of Sigiri, as well as to Ālakamandā , Kuvera and the Sigiri frescoes.

In the days of Parakumba VI (1412 – 1467 AD), says the "Story of Sigiri", an Elder by the name of Vajracharya Buddha Mitra – a great historian and archaeologist came over to Sri Lanka from Swarnapura, embraced the Theravada Sect and later became widely known as the

Elder Ananda. The Elder Ananda, well-versed in Sinhala, Pali, Sanskrit, Greek, Latin and Arabic among other languages, was also an expert in epigraphy. Many historical facts came to light as a result of his researches. These were recorded in lithic inscriptions set up in various places at various times.

The source materials that enabled the Elder Ananda to gather these historical details appear to have been the following:

(a) King Dhatusena's reign: the Dynastic Record
(b) Reign of Kasyapa: the *Suwarnapura Chronicle*
(c) References to Mugalan and Silakala: Ambaheran Salamevan's biography, found in the library of the Great King of Suwarnapura
(d) "*Purana Sinhala Rajavaliya*" (The Chronicle of Ancient Sinhala Kings) which was also the source book for *Culavamsa.*

The Elder Ananda's autobiographical details are followed by a historical description of the days of King Kasyapa. This is based on a hand-book entitled "*Sihigiri Visthara*" (Details of the Lion Rock) in which the relevant historical facts are summarized. (The Story of Sigiri – Preface.)

In this hand-book the historical narrations about King Kasyapa and about Sigiri are set forth thus:

> "After Kasyapa assumed Kingship, Brahmana Maga and the Elder Sankassa of Abhayagiriya had an audience with the King for the second time. The King said that he ascended the Northern face of the Akasa Parvata (The Sky Rock) and examined preliminary work on the Palace his father had planned to build there. He said further that he was contemplating ways and means to raise funds to complete this building project. He said that he had consulted the Architect and the Finance Minister on this matter and requested the advice of Brahmana Maga and Elder Sankassa."

Advising the King about ways and means of raising funds Brahmana Maga says:

> "Send forth a declaration that the King is Kuvera and issue gold coins whose value is guaranteed by the King. The trading community will accept this. As Kuvera is believed to be the Lord of Wealth and the Giver of Wealth, they will never think that any harm will come to them. Since the King rules the land living in a palace atop the rock, the trading community will regard him as Kuvera ". (Chapter VII. Pp. 51 – 58)

Referring to the portraits of ladies, which are part of the city of Kuvera, or Ālākamandā, built with the funds raised through the issue of gold coins, the book says:

"On the side of the rock coated with lime plaster, above the gallery, there are Apsaras, painted in the form of Cloud Damsels and Lightning Princesses". (The Story of Sigiri: Ch. XIV – P. 123.)

This theory advanced by Paranavitana, about the Sigiri Apsaras is also found in his Sigiri Graffiti (Introduction). This was criticized by both art critics and historians. It did not gain general acceptance.

H.C.P.Bell, Sri Lanka's first Commissioner of Archaeology was the pioneer among those who tried to establish the identity of the ladies in the frescoes. The poets of Sigiriya apart, the first scholar to expound a theory about the significance of the Sigiri frescoes was H.C.P.Bell (1897).

His theory was that the ladies in the frescoes represented the queens in Kasyapa's harem who were on their way to Pidurangala Vihara, accompanied by servant maids carrying flowers. He did not even hint that these ladies could be Apsaras even though they are shown as emerging from clouds. At a time when Sigiri lore was not as widely known as it is today and at a time when Sigiri graffiti had not been systematically deciphered, that he should have expressed such a view merits special consideration.

Pidurangala Vihara is situated in the neighbourhood of Sigiriya. The ladies in the Sigiri frescoes, face the Vihara and appear to be walking. They carry flowers. Such considerations could have prompted Bell's theory.

Ananda K. Coomaraswamy concluded that these figures could represent either queens or apsaras, accommpanied by flower-bearing servant maids. (The Arts and Crafts of India and Ceylon. Pg. 83)

One could sum up the views of various scholars who attempted to identify the ladies of the Sigiri frescoes as follows:

(a) They are Queens on their way to Pidurangala Vihara.
H.C.P.Bell – 1897

(b) They are Apsaras floating on clouds.
Ananda K. Coomaraswamy - 1908

(c) They are noble women on their way to a pooja.
Vincent Smith – 1911

(d) They are divine maidens from Tusita heaven.
Havel – 1926

(e) They are heavenly maids taking flowers for a pooja.
Benjamin Roland – 1938

(f) They are Lightning Princesses and Cloud Maidens of Mount Kailasa.
Senerat Paranavitana – 1947

(g) They are Queens of King Kasyapa mourning his death.
Nandadeva Wijesekera – 1959

(h) They are Queens on their way to aquatic sports.
Martin Wickramasinghe

(i) They are the consorts of Bodhisattva Avalokitesvara
Raja de Silva – 1989

In spite of these views and theories, we are still not in a position to establish the identity of the Sigiri ladies, with certainty. Poets who visited Sigiriya and admired the beauty of the Sigiri damsels in the 8th and the 9th centuries faced an identical problem.

We are chronologically about 15 centuries from the time these frescoes were originally executed. But those poets were only 3 or 4 centuries away from that time. Hence, the views they held about the frescoes can be significant. In these poetic compositions, we encounter the Sigiri ladies transformed into aesthetically satisfying images, through the imagination of the poets. The ladies in these poetic compositions are not specific individuals, who could be identified and interpreted as actual historical persons. But they are only artistically created images – that is, exceptionally beautiful works of art. Isn't that exactly what poets usually do?

The preoccupation of the Sigiri poets was with the aesthetic savouring of the beauty of the Sigiri frescoes. These poets infused a new life into these fresco-ladies and viewed them in whatever way they liked through the transforming prism of their poetic imagination.

Perhaps, the poets viewed these fresco-ladies three or four centuries after they appeared on the rock face. Romantic or critical, these comments have a further dimension: they throw light on the customs and social attitudes of a distant day and enrich our knowledge as well as our imagination.

About 40 of these poets, visualised these beauties as ladies of Kasyapa's harem. Each poet sees these queens according to the style and imagination specific to him.

Poet Mahamet says that the golden damsel who (wears) a golden chain on her breast and has a lute in her hand does not speak to anyone else because the king has died. This poem was sung by Laya Sivalu

19 තනරන්-මලී වෙණ අතනි ගත් හො රන්වන් ලි
නිරිඳු මෙළෙන් එකල් නො මෙ බෙ (ණෙය්) අන් නන-හය් යාවත්

Tana-ran-malī veṇa atani gat ho ran-van li
Niridu meḷen ekal no me be[ṇey] an nna hay yāvat

She, the golden-coloured damsel, who (wears) a golden chain on her breast and has taken a lute in her hand, does not speak to anyone else whosoever, as the king died at that time

In lyric 75 another poet thinks that the king had the frescoes painted on the wall and anyone seeing the ladies will speak of the virtues of the king. This lyric consists of two verses which in their subject-matter are not related to each other. Written by the same poet they have been considered as one document.

75. මෙ සෙයි මෙ අඟ්නන් අද්වයි විසි එ නරවරා
අවුද් බැලුයොත් තා කියවි ගුණ එ නරවරා
නැහැජිනැ ඉද් නම් වරජක් මම් කෙළෙම් නම් තිපි
සහව වරජකජ් ඇත මහවත් හෙළිල්ලම්බියෙන්

Me seyi me aṅgan advayi visi e naravarā
Avud bäluyot tā kiyavi guṇa e naravarā
Nähäjinä id nam varajak mam keḷem nam tipi
Sahava varajaka-j äta mahavan heḷillambiyen

In this manner that king had these women painted, and resided (here). If (you) come and look at them, the virtues of that king will be spoken of by you.

If I remain without recognizing (you), and if I committed any fault, may you forbear; even if there be a fault, forgive, O fair damsels.

Dala Siva Himi of Sigama, in lyric 81, says that the damsels are so hard-hearted that, though they enjoyed the company of the King when he was alive, they do not even spare a thought for him after his death.

81. හැ[ජැ]නැ නියළෙන් මයූ කුමට එ මිඳිබියන්
නිරිඳු සෙවැ යෙහෙන් වැසැ නො මළ තද් ළ ඇත සරනට්

Hä[jä]nä niyaḷet mayu kumaṭa e mindibiyan
Niridu sevä yehen väsä no maḷa tad - ḷa äta saranaṭ

Wherefore do these (people) recognize the disdainful ones and grieve (thereby) ? Do they, having associated with the king and lived in happiness, have hearts so hard as not to remember him when he is dead?

One poet condemns them in the guise of praise, saying that they do not even speak a word about the dead King, because of the merit they had acquired in a previous birth which enables them to bear their sorrow stoically.

143. එ මළ ද නො බණය සහනෙ මෙ කිම නම
කළ යි පි න ත පවසමො හිමබ අකමය වය

E maḷa da no baṇaya sahane me kima nama
Kaḷa yi pi na ta pavasamo himaba akamaya vaya

Though (he) is dead, there is endurance (in you), without speaking. What (conduct) is this? We declare that meritorious deeds have been performed by you (in your previous existence). O, my lady, forgive me.

Those very ladies, seen by some poets as possessing admirable self-control befitting royalty, were seen by others as totally bereft of seemly conduct.

Poet Kali, an inmate of the house of King Sen, states that he knows why these ladies have taken shelter in the wilderness and hints at their immoral ways.

63. (සෙන්)රජගෙහි (වැ)සි කළි(යා) ගී
කුමට් දු දන්මො රන්අසර එකත් (වි)සි එක(ල්)
එක(ල්) මෙහි යහවන් තා නො (වි) අසරයට මෙන් තම

(Sen)-raja-gehi (vä)si Kali(yā) gī
Kumaṭ du danmo ran-asara e-kat (vi)si e-ka(l)
E-ka(l) mehi yaha-van tā no (vi) asarayaṭa men tama

We know for what (purpose) that damsel remained in the vicinity of the forest (from) that time. At that time, I trow, you were not there for companionship, in happy manner.

Holding a similar view, Mugalan of Siripura states that they are concealed in the rock-pocket for a nefarious purpose.

65. වැහැවෙත් කිසෙය් බෙයදහි රන්වනුන් දුටුවො
සිවියු(ද) [ෙ]තපුල නැත (උන්) රහසට [නො] බෙයද අතුරෙ [සිටි]
Vähävet kisey beyadahi ran-vanun duṭuvo
Siviyu(da) t[e]pulu näta (un) rahasaṭa [no] beyda ature [siṭi]

In what manner can those who have seen the golden-coloured ones on the mountain side bear themselves up?. Though (they) smiled, there is no speech of them. Is it not for the sake of secrecy that they remained in the midst of the mountain side?

There are some poets who see them simply as courtesans.

111. බිසරියෙ වසැරියුන කලුන ගැණිනයුන සද
බලනනට රිසි [මෙ]ය නො වෙයි බෙයද ගියනට

B[i]sariye vasäriyuna kaluna g[ä]ṇinayuna sada
Balananaṭa risi [m]eya no veyi beyada giyanaṭa

When the damsels are reckoned among those acting in a loose manner, the desire to see this will not be there to those who would have gone to the mountain side.

To the poet a blue-lily complexioned lady is just something to be discarded.

456. අඟ පිරිහිණ් ද දැක්මකුජ් ඇත තමන් හය්
විවැජ්ජු සැප්මුඬු සිකි එ [ම]හනෙල්වන සබද නො

Aṅga pirihiṇ da däkmak=uj äta taman hay
Viväjju säp-muṇḍu siki e [ma]hanel-vana sabada no

Though she is deficient of limbs, she has, nevertheless, a look with her. O friend, that discarded scum of a lily-coloured one is not (suitable for) relationship.

There are also poets who claim that they enjoyed sexual intimacy with these ladies.

460. පතුර්වමි[න්] සනා බස ලත් විඳි සියොව් [සු]ව
මා බඳුවන් ති බැ[ලුව]න් ඇසි මතක් ලී [හ]දහය්

Paturvami[n] sanā basa lat vindi siyov [su]va
Mā banduvan ti bä[luva]n äsi matak lī [ha]dahay
(Your) word, diffusing love, has been obtained and the happiness of union (with you) experienced (by me). What has merely been heard

has been written, having believed it, by those like me who have looked at you.

Like some art-critics of our time, some poets of that day too saw them as Apsaras who had descended to earth. The poet named Sivu is one such. This has a special significance that is not present in other poems which attempt to identify them. It throws light on the manner these aesthetes, poets and other critics expressed their views – interpreting the significance of the Sigiri frescoes, engaging in poetic give-and-take and discussing various issues.

98. මමජ් මෙසෙ[යි]න මෙ උපන් ජැය්හි විසජමි
දී සි[ත්හි එ] සියල් ව[න] සරන් බට් මිහිතෙලෙ

Mama-j me-se[yi]na me upan jäyhi visajami
Dī si[t-hi e] siyal va[n=a]saran baṭ mihi-tele

I, too, in this wise, decide in this matter which has arisen, after having considered in my mind all that (which has been said to me) it is as if heavenly nymphs have descended to the earth.

After considering all the views expressed by those who contemplated the frescoes, the poet concludes that the frescoes depict Apsaras. The suffix 'J' in 'mamaj' (me too) indicates that it is not solely his view. In those days as it is now, there were doubtless controversies about these female figures.

Mindful of the question at issue here, I too will hazard an opinion : they are probably Apsaras who have come down to earth.

It is no wonder that a poet reaching the top of the rock, moved by the breath-taking view of the sky stretching endlessly and surprised by the beauty of the female figures in the rock pocket, should see them as divine maidens. The images used by the poet to express this wonder, heighten the meaning.

178. කිමිජ[බ]රවිල්හි අත්යුගලෙන් ඉගිලී
ගෙලෙ ල විජලි [නි]ව ගිම් දිවඅසර අස (මෙ)හි ආ

Kimij=a[ba]ra-vilhi at-yugalen igilī
Gele la vija-li [ni] va gim diva-asara asa (me)hi ā

Having dived in the lake which is the sky, having flown upwards with the arms (as if with wings), having put on the neck the flashes of lightning and having assuaged the heat, the celestial nymph has come to the vicinity of this place.

Diving in the sky-pool, rising to the air on two wings, wearing garlands of lightning round the neck and quenching the heat the divine maidens arrived here.

Another poet, though not asserting directly that these maidens are divine, states that they have come from heaven. Thus :

644. වස තිදස දැකැ ආ ළඳ පවෙ [ක] ළෙන ගල්තල්
ගමන ඇළ වැ සුළග තොප සැනැහනි මගක් වූ මෙ[න්]

Vasa tidasa däkä ā ḷanda pave [ka]ḷena gal-tal
Gamana äḷa vä suḷaga topa sänähani magak vū me[n]

As the young damsel, who has come (away) after having seen Paradise, made (this) rock her abode, (there is) your going on the surface of the rock, (impelled) by love, bending sideways in the wind, as if it were (along) a road.

It is as if a maiden who had seen Tidaspura in heaven, had taken shelter in the rock. Your walk, impelled by love, avoiding the wind, is like a walk taken along an ordinary road.

She has been to Tidaspura in Heaven. It is as if she had opted to live in the rock-pocket, because it is a better place to live in than even Heaven. The force of love by which she is impelled is so strong that she walks on these difficult rocks as if walking along an ordinary road. This is not an attempt to identify Sigiri maidens. The poet's purpose here is to assert that Sigiri is even lovelier than Tidaspura heaven (that is Tavatimsa Heaven) and that Sigiri maidens seem divine, in their beauty. Still, this seems to uphold indirectly the view held by some poets that Sigiri women are divine maidens.

There are other poems that support the 'Divine Maiden Theory'. But it is unwise to assume without any reservation that these poems unambiguously state that Apsara (heavenly maiden) figures are painted at Sigiriya. It could very well be that the figures seem divine maidens to the poets because of their beauty.

175. සහජ පියනට් නො මෙය්හි සරන් (අඳ්)ව තු [බු]
[දිගැ]ස්නි අ සෙය් ගනු සඳ්පහනට් සුළග් මඳ් වනන්

Sahaja piyanaṭ no meyhi saran (and)va tu[bu]
[Digä]sni a sey ganu sand-pahanaṭ suḷag mand vann

Is it not for the sake of born lovers that nymphs have been painted here? O long-eyed ones, take the manner (in which I have) come, to be similar to (the coming of) the gentle breeze to the moonlight.

Have these maidens not been painted here for those who always love them? You long-eyed ones, please accept, therefore, union between you and me, like the combination of moonlight with a gentle breeze.

The Sigiri poets do not share Paranavitana's view that the golden-hued maidens represent lightning but they too see the golden-hued maidens as resembling lightning.

192. දැකැ තර් නිවය් කිසෙය්නි සිත්වර් සා ලළයුන්
බෙයන්ද් කිසැ සහරා විජ්ලියවන්වූ වරඟනන්

Däkä tar nivay kiseyni sit-var sā lalayun
Beyand kisä saha-rā vij-liya-van-vū varaṅganan

Having seen the lovely, noble damsels in the interior of the mountain side – (damsels) who are comparable to the glittering lightning - how does the painter assuage (his) great affliction?

Seeing the comely maidens in the rock-pocket, who resemble many-hued lightning, how does the artist suppress his deep sorrow?

While the artist painted these maidens and was engaged in depicting their perfect feminine charm, he was at one with them in his world of imagination. But does it not give him a sense of deep sorrow, to feel that at the end of that intimate identification with these beauties, he has to leave them to the King?

Many expressions of poetic thought compare the golden maidens to lightning. But they appear to be merely poetic fancies and cannot be construed as evidence linking Sigiri with Ālakamandā. Poet Kitala from Mahana-vutu says:

555. විදුකි[ද] මත [ඇ] ති ද එබිමො [දි]සි තක් දි[ටි] වී
වියෙවුන් බඳුන් බෙයදිහි රන්[වනු]න් නො [මෙ වී] බුණ

Vidu-ki[da] mata [ä]ti da ebimo [di]si tak di[ṭi] vī
Viyevun band=un beyadihi ran-[vanu]n no [me vī] buṇa

We peeped (to see) whether there was a streak of lightlning above, (and then), was seen all that is worth seeing, (namely) the golden-coloured ones who stood on the mountain side, without speaking, in the manner of those separated (from their lovers).

The poet visited the rock-pocket, but was unaware that there were maidens there. He was able to see them only when he tried to find out how a flash of lightning appeared in the rock-pocket. This is a remarkable instance of poetic suggestion or evocation (*dhvani*) created to bring out the beauty of the golden figures of the maidens.

Some poets saw these maidens as the queens of the King, but to some they were the women of the King's harem. The poet-monk Sirina from Taralpa was one of them.

147. තරල්පාවැසි සිරිනාපැවිජෙජමි
නිරිද්සිරැ සිටැ බැහැරට් නො [ෙ]ම යම පරවිටි
එවන් වී නැවතැ බලමි[න්*] සිටියවුන් වැන්නො

Taral-pā-väsi Sirinā-pävijjemi
Nirid-sirä siṭä bähäraṭ no m[e] yama paraviṭi
E-van vī näväta balami[n*] sitiyavun vänno

'Having lived in the King's harem, we shall certainly not go outside in his absence'. Thus reflecting, they are as if they have stopped and are standing, looking (forward).

It is as if they stayed put, where they were, waiting for the King, firmly resolved: "we of the King's harem will never go out without his permission, turning our backs on him."

They are the women of the King's harem. They do not want to go counter to the accepted norms of behaviour by going out in the absence of the King. They firmly believe that the King will come back. Therefore, they stay put, waiting for him to return.

They are beauties in front of the poet who scrawled the poem:

417. එ රජ්හු අඟ්නක් [බැලීමො] ආ අප [ඇ]ස්නි
බලමින් හෙර් සෙයින් බණ[න්නි] අත්[නෙන්] ආ හය්

E raj[1]hu aṅgnak [bälīmo] ā apa [ä]sni
Balamin her seyin baṇa[nni] at[nen] ā hay

We, who came here, looked at a damsel of that king with our (own) eyes. Looking at (them) in the manner of a roguish woman, she speaks with those who came here by means of her hands.

These Sigiri maidens who are stunningly beautiful even today would have exerted a hypnotic power over the poets, thousands of years ago, when the frescoes were fresh and brighter.

Poet Piyal believes that these are the King's consorts.

124. වනවූ දිගැස්සන් නරනින්‍දහු දුක්මැස්සන්
පියල් බැලි අවුජ් බෙයන්‍දහී පුල්නිල්උපුල්ඇස්සන්

Vanavū digässan naranind'hu duk-mässan
Piyal bäli avuj beyand'hī pul-nil-upul-ässan

Piyal, having come (here) ,saw on the mountain side the long-eyed (women) who are separated (from their lover), who are grieving for the sufferings of the king, and who possess eyes (like unto) full-blown 'lue lilies.

As do the art-critics of today, the poets of those days, too, made an effort to establish the identity of the Sigiri ladies. Yet, even today their identity is an unsolved mystery. May it remain unsolved for ever! May these Sigiri ladies continue to rouse emotions in viewers for ages to come. May their identity continue to create curiosity and may they bear witness only to the perfection of the feminine form.

Monk Sirina of Taralpa Pirivena, observing the intimacy poets had with the maidens of Sigiri offers a piece of advice. He raises the echo of a warning, saying, "Do you not know that these paintings were left behind by the King?".

130. මෙසෙය් මෙ සව්සතු සියොව්සිරී විද් ද වී
තබය් පිළිබිබ් රජු යිහි මෙ ගියයුන් නොජත් සෙය් කිම්
තරල්පා පිරිවෙන්වැසි සිරිනා පැවිජෙජ [මි] සිතීම්

Me-sey me sav-satu siyov-sirī vid da vī
Tabay pilibib raju yihi me giyayun nojat sey kim
Taralpā-piriven-väsi Sirinā-pävijje[mi] sitīm

Though all these people, in this manner, enjoyed the good fortune of union (with loved ones), (they), it seems, have not known that the king departed, having left here these pictures. Why (is that)?

It seems that they are not aware that the King left these images here. It may be a warning of dire consequences one has to face for intimacy with royal women.

Does the poet-monk state, on historical evidence available at that time, that the King had these paintings done.Or is it merely a poetic fantasy?

Kital – a resident of Abalava in the western region holds an identical view.

206. නොඑක් ජන අර්බය් හසර හෙළිලලබුයු න
ඇජ තබයි පිළිබිබ් (අහො) ගියෙ රජ කතුන් රස කොට

Noek jana arbay hasara heḷillabuyu na
Äja tabayi piḷibib (aho) giye raja katun rasa koṭa

Alas! The King departed, having tastefully painted and left on the path the pictures of the lovely fair damsels for the sake of diverse (sorts of) persons.

The poet says the King departed, leaving behind by the way side, the images of the beauties for the pleasure of the masses.

Poem 247 creates a new impression by portraying these as desperate in sorrow:

247. බෙයඳ්හි රන්වනු නිරිඳ්[ඉ]සිරා වියෙව්හි
මෙසිනි මියහෙම්හ යි ගල්ඇගැනි හෙනයුන් වැන්නො

Beyand'hi ran-vanu nirind-[i]sirā viyevhi
Mesini miyahemha yi gal-ägäni henayun vänno

The golden-coloured ones on the mountain side have the appearance of those hurling themselves (down) from the summit of the rock, (saying) 'we shall die', out of grief in (their) separation from (their) lord, the king.

These maidens who have climbed to the edge of the Sigiri rock seem to be poised to jump off the cliff and kill themselves unable to bear separation from the King.

217. නො වී ලද බස[කු]ද් දෙක [ම]ල් අත රන් වනුන්
මෙ ගී සෙල නෙගි හිඳි බඳ් හිමියා පෙරෙ මෙළෙන් තම

No vī lada basa[k=u]d deka [ma]l ata ran -vanun
Me gī sela negi hindi band himiyā pere meḷen tama

Though not having received even a word (from them), having seen the flowers in the hands of the golden- coloured ones, this was sung – (the golden-coloured ones) who, as it were,stand (there) having ascended the rock, as their lord died in former days.

Though he does not receive even one word from these maidens, the poet scrawls a poem moved merely by the sight of flowers in their hands. But, to no avail. The poet knows why. It is not his fault. They have climbed to the top of the rock bereaved of their consort. This is hardly the time for pleasant words.

The poet who composed lyric number 109 says:

109. බැලූමො ගිරිබිතැ ළකොළ් හෙළිල්ලම්බුයුන්
කො ජ ගියෙ හිමිය යි බලම් සිටියුයුන් වැන්නො

Bälūmo giri-bitä ḷa-koḷ heḷillambuyun
Ko ja giye himiya yi balam siṭiyuyun vänno

We looked at the heart-shattering fair damsels on the rock wall. They seemed as if they stood (there) looking (forward, wondering) where their lord had gone.

"As if waiting for the consort". is a statement that tugs at the heart of those sensitive viewers.

If these figures represent maidens mourning the death of the King, obviously they were done after the King's death and not before. But one must not forget that this too is a poetic fancy. Mital, one of the poets resorting to this fantasy expresses a fresh view.

446. හිමි දැකැ [සිත්]හි කිපි වි ද ගිරිහිස නැගි එකල
පිනු ලු ගිරි(හිසි)න් තොප මල්පලු පලන් සෙ කොලොබ

Himi däkä [sit]'hi kipi vi da giri-hisa nägi e-kala
Pinu lu giri-(hisi)n topa mal-palu palan se koloba

Was it having seen your lord, enraged in mind, that you, at that time, got up to the summit of the rock? They say that you leaped down from the summit of the rock like a koloba (tree), bedecked with flowers and sprays.

Seing the king – their consort - angry, they climbed to the top of the rock and jumped off the cliff like a 'koloba' tree.

This does not refer to a separation from the King. It is because of the King's ire. The poets of Sigiri never solved the enigma whether the Sigiri rock was decked by real maidens or by maidens called up by the artist's imagination. May it remain a secret like a mystery enshrined in a heart.

If the Sigiri damsels are Kasyapa's consorts or other historical personages they would be of limited importance and of little significance. If they represent artistic creations, however, their significance would be limitless. For unlike in the world of reality, in the world of art what is important acquires a universal significance. The Sigiri damsels, as artistic creations, indeed provide a glimpse of the eternal female.

FLOWERS IN THEIR HANDS - SYMBOLS OF LOVE?

Many Sigiri lyrics reveal that the flowers in the hands of the Sigiri damsels have fascinated many a poet. They suggest that flowers symbolized love during Sigiri times. It is possible that lovers of all times expressed their feelings through flowers.

Even among the Jataka tales in Buddhist literature, which naturally have a definite religious bias, there are stories with love as the central theme. But do we get any information about symbols of love from these stories?

Sigiri poets assuredly say that the flowers in the hands mean much more than what was expressed in words.

310. අනඳ සති පෙරෙටු යහ අයිහ (දෙක)හි
වීසි මහනෙලවනනි මල බලගන කළ තිපි
රනහලපිරිවෙනව(ැ)සි අනඳපැවිජන ගී විසඳනෙ

Ananda sati pereṭu yaha ayiha (deka)hi
Visi mahanela-vanani mala bala-gana kaḷa tipi
Ranahala-pirivena-v(ä)si Ananda-p(ä)vijana gī visandane

O lily-coloured ones, (you) who remained here, with joy and mindfulness to the fore in happiness and unhappiness, you have been created by having looked at a flower.

The above verse by Monk Ananda, suggests that the women here are modelled after flowers : *'mala balagana kala tipi'* (you have been created by having looked at a flower). Women here symbolize flowers and the flowers they present to their viewers in turn represent themselves, i.e., their love for them. In a society where chastity and self-respect were the highest ideals of womanhood, the flowers they offer symbolize their purity and comeliness as well as a suffusion of love.

Apart from the fact that the poets believed that the damsels expressed their love in general through the flowers held in their hands, there is no room for us to infer from the creations of these poets that flowers of various species or the position the flowers are held in the hands convey any particular idea or emotion. Although the poetic concepts of the Sigiri poets, inspired by the flowers in the hands of 'speechless' damsels, do not symbolize love, poet Buyuru Kasaba of the house of Lord Sena, a resident of Gaduba–vana reveals how the damsels spoke with flowers in the following lyric.

187. (ගැඩුබ)වනවැසි සෙනහිමියන ගෙ බුයුරු කසබා ගෙ ගී
රතඅත පලු(ම)ලෙන අබුළ ළපතක සෙයි ලි මෙ
[බිණි]වි සැබ[වින] හිමබුයු නොබණනනො කී නොවදන

(Gäḍuba)-vana-väsi Sena-himiyana ge Buyuru Kasabā ge gī
Rata-ata palu-[ma]lena abuḷa ḷa-pataka seyi li me
[Biṇi]vi säba[vina] himabuyu no-baṇanano kī no-vadana

This damsel, like unto a fluttering tender bud, in fact spoke with the buds and flowers in her hand; it is (therefore) an untrue word that has been said: 'The ladies do not speak'.

Paranavitana interprets 'Palu-(ma) lena (bini) vi' as 'spoke with the buds and flowers'.

We may take it that, the silence of the damsels was no deficiency in the eyes of the poets because the damsels did express their feelings with flowers. Probably the poets thought that even the mildest words were too harsh a medium to express the tenderness of feelings of love. Expression of love that cannot be captured in words was achieved not with intangible, unseen words but with flowers. Poet Vijurala – bata writes:

642. [ගල්]තෙලෙහි ඇඳි මෙය හජ[නා නුයුන්] කො[ට] මන
නො බැ[ණැ සි]ටී ජත ද මා සිත ඇදි වි [ගත්]තෙන් මල් වි[ජුර] ලබතිමි ලීමි

[Gal]-telehi ändi meya haja[nā nuyun] ko[ṭa] mana
No bä[ṇä si]ṭī jata da mā sita ädi vi [gat]ten mal
Vi[jura]la-batimi līmi

Though it was known by me that this (lady), who has been painted on the surface of the rock so as to attract (one's) eyes, stands here without speaking (her) mind, (my) mind was drawn (to her) as flowers are taken (by her).

The poet Sivala of Hedigam gets the damsel in the painting to confess that flowers in her hands expressed what was in her mind:

439. හෙඩි[ග]ම් සිවලැ ගී
අප මන ජ[තුන් සෙය් ඔ]යුන අ වියි මලනි තම
සෙ ඇ[ති] හෙළි විනි [බැ]ලිමි බිතු වසන්නට මෙසෙ ගත

Heḍi[ga]m Sivalä gī
Apa mana ja[tun sey o]yuna a viyi malani tama
Se ä[ti] heḷi vini [bä]limi bitu vasannaṭa mese gata

'Ah! What is in our minds has, it seems, been known by them by means of our flowers,' When the wall, in this manner, has been taken (by you) to reside (on), I saw the manner in which what is (in your minds) has been revealed.'

When the damsel confesses – 'Ah what is in our minds has been known by them by means of our flowers, the poet (the visitor) replies: 'Yes, you yourself are to be blamed for this because you have taken up your abode on the wall.'

It is not only the flowers that express what is in her mind. The poet suggests that the damsel had taken up her abode in a concealed place such as this because she is keeping a secret in her mind. What is significant in this song is that the poet gets the damsels themselves to confess that they express their love with flowers.

27. අප බස එවැන්නෙක් ඇසුවෙ ද හළෙ මෙ දස් වී
හිමි තම මළ සිවි තමා දත් ද කී අත මල් ගත්

Apa basa e-vännek äsuve da haḷe me das vī
Himi tama maḷa sivi tamā dat da kī ata mal gat

The above poem tells of a man who became a slave to a woman with flowers in hands although her husband was dead.

Paranavitana interprets this:

Having become a slave to this (wench), one like that, though he heard our speech, rejected it – (our speech) which said, 'Did you know that she, who has taken flowers in her hand, smiled (even) when her Lord is dead?'

One poet climbed Sigiri thinking that he could see Heaven from its summit. But what he really saw was much more attractive - flowers in the ladies' hands. He says he became insane. To evoke such feelings the flowers should have been of a special significance, suggestive and full of life. The purpose of these flowers was to express feelings of love to attract the minds of men.

The following lyric is a case in point:

429. සග දිසි සිතා මෙහි බලමින් අයුතින් බෙයඳ්
දිගැසින් අත මල් (දැකැ) මනමත් කෙ ද නොවන්නො

Saga disi sitā mehi balamin ayutin beyand
Digäsin ata mal (däkä) mana-mat ke da no-vanno

Having come here, thinking that the Heaven is to be seen, and looking at the mountain side, who do not become maddened in mind, (after) having seen the flowers in the hands of the long-eyed ones?

Seeing the ladies with flowers in their hands on the Sigiri rock, the poets were enthralled by a splendour greatly exceeding that found in Heaven. Notwithstanding the fact that the ladies expressed themselves with flowers, one poet makes a plea that he be favoured with at least one word.

597. ළද[ඔ]යු[න්] වී ගත් ද නො වැහැවෙය් නො ළද් වී
දිග්නෙතුනි තෙපලක් දෙවු ඇති ද ගෙ[නැ ම]ල් ත[ම] අ[ත]

Lada [o]yu[n] vī gat da no vähävey no lad vī
Dig-netuni tepalak devu äti da ge[nä ma]l ta[ma] a[ta]

"Do you think you have obtained them?" "Not having obtained (them), I am unable to bear myself up". "O long-eyed ones, do give a word, even though flowers have been taken in your hands".

However much the poets loved the Sigiri ladies they could not get even one word in response from them. So the poets in frustration did not hesitate to regard them as disdainful. But poet Mihind of the house of Lord Kasub comes to their defence:

650. දි[ගැස්] මල් අතැ [ගත්] බල[මින්] කෙසෙ මිඬිබි කී
ඇවිද් මෙ හිඬි ලී බෙයඬ් බලනෙය් රිසි කොට් තමා
.... වැසි කසුබ්හිමියන් ගෙ මිහිඬ්මි මෙ ගී ලීමි

Di[gäs] mal atä [gat] bala[min] kese mindibi kī
Ävid me hindi lī beyand balaney risi koṭ tamā
.... väsi Kasub-himiyan ge Mihindmi me gī līmi

Looking at the long-eyed one who has taken flowers in her hand, how has it been said (that she is) a disdainful one? Having come to this, the damsel who remained on the mountain side should be looked at by you with pleasure.

It is wrong for the poets to call these ladies disdainful just because they do not speak. Although they do not speak, do they not express themselves fully with the flowers held in their hands? To assure oneself one may climb the rock and look at the ladies with pleasure.

Poet Bata says:

588. (ඇ)ඬි(යෙන් මෙ) සිතුවර් ග[ත්] මෙ[න් මල්] අතින් තොප
දිසි සෙ[ය්] සග [වී] බෙයඬ් දිසි අමබු සෙය් මි[ඬි] බි නො වි

(Ä)ndi(yen me) situvar ga[t] me[n mal] atin topa
Disi se[y] saga [v ī]beyand disi ambu sey mi[ndi]bi no vi

The painter has drawn you as having taken flowers in (your) hand; the mountain side, therefore, appeared as if it were heaven, and the woman appeared as if she were not a disdainful one.

683. ගත් හිද ගල් සෙයින් ම තද මෙහි ඇය බණතුද්
මෙසෙයි මෙහි හිද ගතතින් මහනෙල්හි ඇති සුවඳින්

Gat hida gal seyin ma tada mehi äya baṇat=ud
Me-seyi mehi hida gat=atin mahanelhi äti suvandin

(Her) heart has been taken by me here (to be) as hard as stone, even though she, having stood here in this manner, speaks (to me) with the fragrance which is there in the water-lily taken in her hand.

Poet Mihidal is not satisfied although the damsel spoke to him with the fragrance which is there in the water-lily, taken in her hand. He believes that although she speaks with the fragrance of the water-lily, her heart is as hard as stone.

One poet asks another:

649. මොළො(කතින්) ගෙනැ [ම]ල් [බ]ලය් මෙ බෙ[ය]ඳැහි [හිඳි]
මීලැස්සන් සිහිගිරි අවෙ කිම ද නො ලදින් තා

Moḷo(katin) genä [ma]l [ba]lay me be[ya]ndahi [hindi]
Mīlässan Sihigiri ave kima da no ladin tā

Wherefore did you come (away), without having obtained the deer-eyed ones of Sihigiri – (they) who stood, gazing (forward) on the mountain side, having taken flowers in their tender hands?

These ladies keep gazing at you with tender flowers in their hands. And if they have flowers in their hands one could certainly obtain their love. If so, why does he return without obtaining the deer-eyed one? The sneer implied in the question is that he is unworthy of her love.

Although she carried flowers in her hands, her love was only for a select few, not for all. Song 581 is a gentle admonition to a woman carrying flowers. It suggests that flowers are a symbol of love.

581. වී සෙ[ර මො] මෙනියා කළ වී [ද] මො මෙනියා
අන්නට් මල් අ[ත්නි ගති] මට් ගලැ [කළ] සෙ වී තද

Vī se[ra mo] me-niyā kala vī[da] mo me-niyā
Annaṭ mal a[tni gati] maṭ galä [kaḷa] se vī tada

Was this (woman) roguish to this extent? Did this (woman, indeed) act in this manner? For others, (she) has taken flowers in her hand. For me, (she) was as hard as if she were made of stone.

The poet's hopes had been so high that he is shocked: "Why was she roguish? Why did she do this to me?"

Poet Mihidala says:

214. (දිගි)ලි කිතලමලනගෙ මි[හි]දලමි (මෙ මය්) ගී
තොප අතැ ගත් මහනෙලමලින් මලක් අ(ප හට)
නො මෙ [දු] [න්] හෙ [යින්]කුම් සෙයි ඇති බස ස(නා තෙ) [ප]ල(ය්)

(Digi)li Kitala-malanage Mi[hi]dalami (me may) gī
Topa atä gat mahanela-malin malak a(pa-hata)
No me [du] [n] he[yin] kum seyi äti basa sa(nā te) [pa]la(y)

A flower out of the blue water-lilly flowers taken in your hands has not been given to us. Therefore, in what manner (can it be said) that words of love have been uttered?

She carries flowers in her hand as a symbol of a word of affection; any woman carrying flowers in her hands symbolically implies words of love. Like the women the poet himself is well aware of this convention. But he ignores the convention and refuses to acknowledge that she has uttered a word of love. To acknowledge that she did express her love, the poet wants her to give a flower that she carries in her hands to him.

One doe-eyed damsel, although she is aware that the poet is near her, pretends not to have seen him. But he is not offended. Why? Because she has taken blue-lily flowers in her rosy hands which suggests that she is prepared to offer her love to him.

655. බෙයඳ් හිඳි මීලැ[සි] වී දුට් නොජත්තන් සෙය්
රතන් [නි]ලුපුල ම[ල් ග]ත් [වී]යින් අපට් තොස් දිනි

Beyand hindi mīlä[si] vī duṭ no-jattan sey
Rat=at [ni]l=upula ma[l ga]t [vī]yin apaṭ tos dini

The deer-eyed one, who remained on the mountain side, as if she has not recognized (us) (even though) having seen (us), gave pleasure to us as she has taken blue lotus flowers in (her) rosy hand.

A poet writing a song about a lady not carrying flowers in her hands puts forward an idea like this:

669. මෙහි හි[ඳි] හෙළිල්ල[ඹු] ත කී සෙ[ය්] වෙ[න්න]ක් නො [වෙ]
[ග]ත නො වී [ද] මො මල් අතින් මෙ[බ]ඳු දුට් [සැ] ඳැ තුට් [සිත]

Mehi hi[ndi] heḷilla[mbu] ta kī se[y] ve[nna]k no [ve]
[Ga]ta no v ī[da] mo mal atin me-[ba]ndu duṭ[sä]ndä tuṭ [sita]

The fair damsel who remained here is not one who is of the sort spoken of by you. Though this one has not taken flowers in her hand, when one like this is seen, the mind is rejoiced.

It is the doe-eyed ones who always pleased the poets. Although they do not speak, they express themselves with flowers. So how could one say that a lady having no flowers in her hands pleased a poet?

A friend of the poet has made a comment about this lady with which he doesn't agree. He insists that this lady 'is not of the sort' spoken of by him. What could have been the friend's comment?

Probably the friend had commented that the lady was a hard-hearted, disdainful one having no flowers in her hands to receive the poet.

What is the poet's reply : "I don't mind this beautiful one not uttering words of love to me and not carrying flowers in her hands. Although she doesn't favour me with her love, seeing a beautiful lady like her stimulates my mind".

This song written about a lady having no flowers in her hands shows that carrying flowers was a special symbol of love.

The following song reveals that the mere carrying of flowers does not satisfy the poets:

662. [ර]ත් අතිනි මල් ගෙ[නැ] හෙළිල්ලඹු සිටි ම[න] මය්
පිරිබුන් මඳ [බැ]වින් සිහිගිරි [නැ] ගියෙ මත මි[නිසන]

[Ra]t atini mal ge[nä] heḷillambu siṭi ma[na] may
Piribun manda [bä]vin Sihigiri [nä]giye mata mi[nisana]

As it is not enough that my heart was shattered by the fair damsel who, having taken flowers in her rosy hands, stood (here), men climbed to the summit of Sihigiri.

The poet is at a loss to understand why other men climbed to the summit whereas his heart has been shattered by the damsel.

Having flowers in her hands is a definite sign that a damsel is in love. With this conviction the poet pursued her but, his love being not requited as expected, his heart was shattered.

Flowers are beautiful; fragrant. They are so enchanting as to attract bees from afar. Is it a surprise that the poets were enamoured by seeing these beautiful, fragrant flowers in the hands of the Sigiri damsels?

Many a poet, as already observed, has seen flowers as a symbol of love. Here the poet finds fault with the damsels for taking flowers in their hands:

36. නැගී බැලූමො මීලැස්න එ ත ගී
සුරතත්හි මල්දම් නො හො[බි]යි කිසි සිලූ රන්වන්

Nägī bälūmo mīläsna e ta gī
Surat=at'hi mal-dam no ho[bi]yi kisi silū ran- van

We ascended (the rock) and looked at those deer-eyed ones who have been sung about by you. It is in no wise becoming that the golden coloured ones have taken garlands of flowers in their exceedingly rosy hands

Although there is no indication here that the husband of this damsel is dead the poet obviously chides her for taking flowers, a symbol of love, in her hands even after her husband's death. Even verse 27, which was earlier discussed, suggests that it is unbecoming of women to take flowers in their hands after the death of their husbands. As a reply to this accusation one poet speaks in defence of women as follows:

33. මෙ පළ [ද] වරද ලෙද ම නො ගත් කී වදන් තා
අතින් [ගිලි හුණ] මල් ගත් මෙළෙන් වරල මුදත් [හිමි]

Me paḷa [da] varada leda ma no gat kī vadan tā
Atin [gili huṇa] mal gat meḷen varala mudat [himi]

Paranavitana interprets this poem as:

Though this is well known to be a transgression, the words spoken by you have (nevertheless) not been accepted by me. She has merely taken in her hand the flowers which dropped down, when she loosened her hair as her lord died.

Here the poets find fault with these damsels for taking flowers in their hands deeming it a symbol of love. But they are in fact not guilty of such an offence. They have merely picked up the flowers which dropped down when they loosened their hair when their husbands died. For what offence then, are they being blamed?

This verse also reveals that holding flowers had been conventionally regarded in Sigiri society as a token of love.

The poets, thinking that the damsels were offering their love because they were carrying flowers in their hands, had written appealing verses and made a vain attempt to win their love. To them poet Devala of Galaboyi offers this advice:

678. මෙ රන්ව[න්] මලිසිලු වි ජු අද් තබය් හිමියා
කෙරෙන් සත් ජන්මයෙහිජ් වියො නො වෙන්නන් වැනි වී
යහපත්මි අය්හ නැත්ත් උකැටිලි ම [දෙ]සෙ නැත්ත් හෙය්නි
අත්හෙය්නි අත් හෙයින් වනය නො දක්නෙ න් මතෙත

Me ran-va[n] mal=isilu vi ju ad tabay himiyā
Keren sat janmayehi-j viyo no vennan väni vī
Yahapatmi ayha nätt ukäṭili ma [de]se nätt heyni
At=heyni at heyin vanaya no dakne n matte

This golden-coloured one, though she carries flowers, was like one who does not become separated from (her) lord even in seven (future) births, let alone today.

I am one who has attained happiness. There is no unhappiness (in me), for the reason that there is no despondency in my quarter. (This again is), by not seeing (any good) that will come to be in the future by reason of being possessed of the shrinking of one's own self.

Although it is stated that these damsels would not be separated even in seven future births, the fact that the poet concedes that taking of flowers in their hands is a token of love is affirmed by his statement – 'mal-isilu vi ju', "though (she) carried flowers."

Let us now turn from the ladies to the poets who wrote of them.

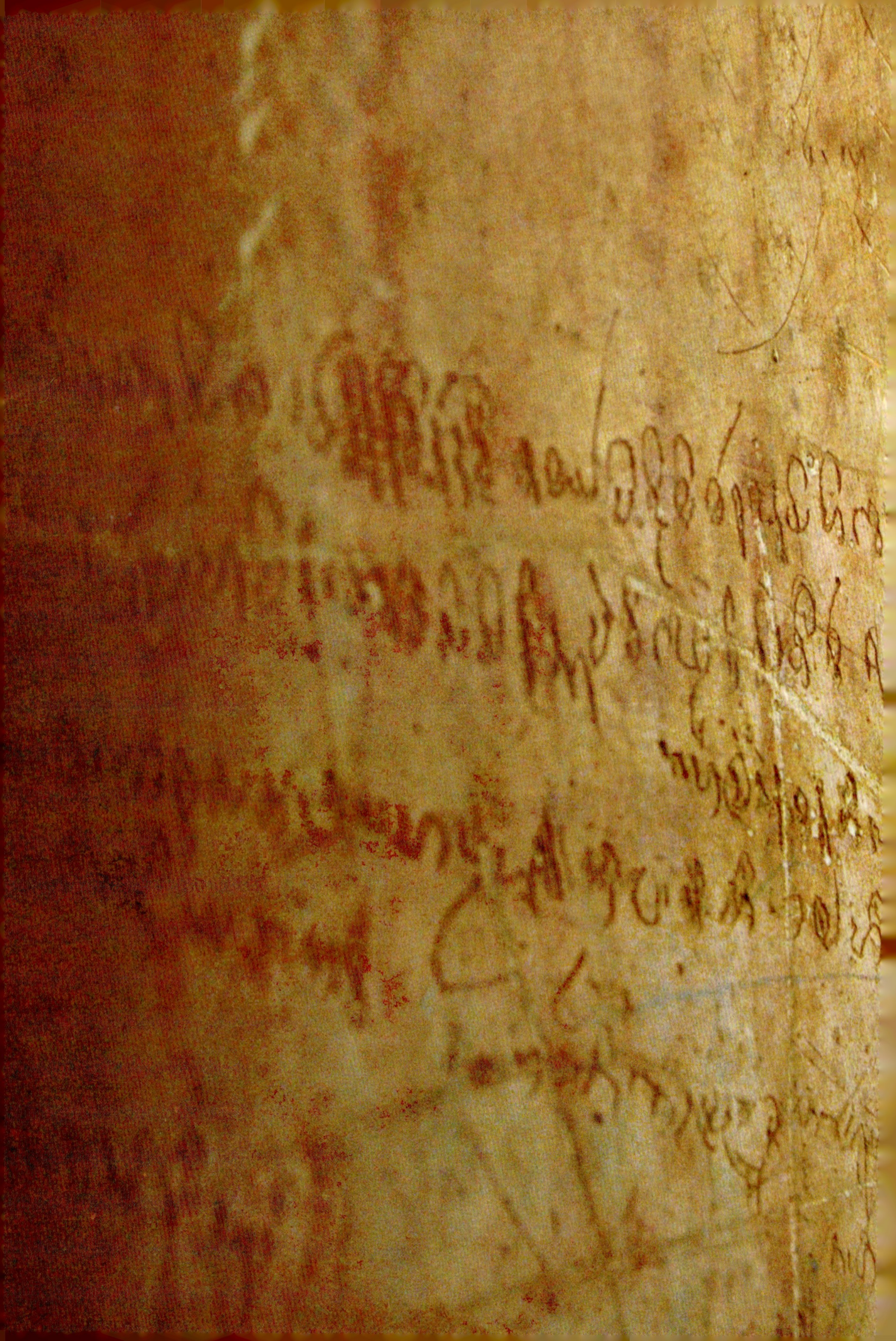

SONGS ON THE MIRROR WALL AT SIGIRIYA

Sigiriya is not as lofty as Pidurangala or Rahangala, nor is it as holy as Samantakuta or Mihintale. However at Sigiriya, located in the Inamaluva Korale of the Matale District, is an art gallery which attracts visitors not only from the four corners of Sri Lanka but also from all over the world.

At Sigiriya are representations of maidens referred to as the "blue coloured ones" (*nilvanun*) and "golden ones" (*ranvanun*) by the Sigiriya poets, and as "cloud damsels" (*meghalata*) and "lightning damsels" (*vijjukumari*) by Professor Paranavitana. They are of lasting significance in the history of art. The lyrics of the Sigiriya graffiti, which are an outcome of the aesthetic appeal of the painted figures, merit a place of the highest honour as distinctive emotive literary creations, not only of Sri Lanka but also of the rest of the world.

Of the many thousands who have visited Sigiriya, a few have immortalized themselves, and it is as though their voices are being heard, and their heart-beat felt by us even now. It is possible to sense the delicacy of their thought, their wisdom and their mental discipline. On the Mirror Wall at Sigiriya they left the reflection of their characters in he emotive verses referred to above. Paranavitana deciphered nearly 700, and supplied meanings and exegeses to them. The results of this exercise have shed much light on the study of the literature, art and history of those times, and have inspired connoisseurs to view the paintings from many different perspectives.

In these lyrics the Sigiriya poets have provided us with an object lesson in the use of suggestion, or '*dhvani*' the most admired figure of speech as in Anandvardhana's Dhvanyaloka.

The references to bodily posture, glance, smile, dress and ornaments and the symbols expressing love are so inter-woven with literary embellishments that meanings not evident superficially are conveyed to us by suggestion. Those who do not understand the Sigiriya lyrics, but yet obtain aesthetic pleasure by viewing the Sigiriya paintings, could double their pleasure by understanding the verses.

As we look at the damsel with a <u>sapu</u> flower in her hand (S. Paranavitana, <u>Sigirya Graffiti</u>, Oxford, 1956/313), we perceive how clearly the artist has delineated her features with the use of soft colours. Normally our attention is not focused on anything beyond the appreciation of external beauty, but this particular poet has revealed to us even her psyche and brought her to life. He seems to engage us in a friendly dialogue with her.

313. අතට [හො] අ මෙන් සුරත්අත්ති ගත් සපුමල්
[කැ]නෙන් නහම් ගතහෙ ජ මන ගත්තී මුළුල්ලෙන්
අග්බො[යි සෙන්]මි

Ataṭ [ho] a men surat-atni gat-sapu-mal
[kä]nen naham gata-he ja mana gattī muḷullen
Agbo[yi Sen]mi

She has taken, in her rosy hand, a <u>sapu</u> flower as if it had come (by itself) to her hand. (She) is unable to take it from the cluster; yet she has taken my mind in its entirety.

It is, thus, with a new approach inspired by the words of this poet, Agboyi Sen, that we begin to look at this particular fresco. He creates in us a feeling that we are actually looking at a living damsel with human consciousness and not merely at a lifeless portrait. As archaeologists and historians search for the meaning of the damsels, the poet transports us to a world of aesthetic pleasure and enjoyment.

The lyrics datable to the 8th and the 9th centuries portray the enthusiasm with which the common man of the times ascended Sigiriya. The poets themselves have left evidence that they were encouraged to do so not merely by the damsels in the frescoes or the beauty of the environment but also because of other concerns.

174. (අ)[වු](ද්) මුළු වෙ ගිරිහි යන වී අප මුළු විසිරි
[සි]හිඳුන් සෙය හැඟැ අප සිහි වන්නට් සිහිගිරි

(A)[vu](d) muḷu ve girihi yana vī apa muḷu visiri
[Si]hid=un seya hä(ṅ)gä apa sihi vannaṭ Sihigirī

Having come here, (the people) become crowded (together) on the rock. The lord of lions, it seems, felt (this)and stood (here)in order that we may scatter ourselves from the crowd and go away, and also to secure that Sihigiri shall be impressed on our memory.

Poet Vajur Agboy residing in the house of Lady Sata says:

286. [සා]තාකලු ගෙ වසන වජුර් අග්බොය්මි
ගල්මුඳුන් නැගී බැලීමි බෙයඳ මා සිත්
රෙපෙ දුන් මගුල් කෙළෙමි සීහිමියා බැලැනි වී

[Sā]tākalu ge vasana Vajur Agboymi
Gal-mundun nägī bälīmi beyandä mā sit
Repe dun magul keḷemi sī-himiyā bäläni vī

I ascended the summit of the rock and looked at (things). On the mountain side I celebrated festivities which (as it were) gave form to my thoughts. All this came to pass through the might of His Majesty the Lion.

289. බෙයද නැගී මෙ ගැයු[ම්]නි ත වැයිමෙ
ය[ද]ම් ඇලී නැග සිටි[මී] සිතී සිකි රනවන

Beyada nägī me gäyu[m]ni ta väyime
Ya-[da]m älī näga siṭi[mī] sitī siki rana-vana

When you, having ascended this mountain side, play music (accompanied) with singing, the golden-coloured one, O friend, thought: 'I shall climb up clinging on to the iron chain and remain (there);
Poet Kottami in his lyric says:

299. නැගි සිසි සඳ බලය් බසි[ත] සඳ්හන කොට [ම]න
නෙ[ත්] නිල් මී[ලැස්න] පිළිදි ජොත්ත සිහි විනි

Nägi sisi sanda balay bas[ita] sand'hana koṭa[ma]na
Ne[t] nil mī[läsna] piḷi-d[ī] jotta [s]ihi v[ī]n[ī]

When (I) climb down, having looked at (this) when the moon had arisen, and having kept in my mind the blue eyes of the deer-eyed ones, the light of a crystal lamp came to my mind.

Lord Samana says:

382. මෙයට එන මදනල වල්විජ්නා සියලෙලනි
සෙයි මෙ අය් (ග)ත ලියයුන ග(ල්)බෙයද ආ මු(දුන)ට

Meyaṭa ena mada-nala val-vijnā siyalleni
Seyi me ay (ga)ta liyayuna ga(l)-beyada ā mu(duna)ṭa

The gentle breeze which comes to this (place) is as if it came to this from all the (yak)-tail fans taken (in their hands) by the ladies who have come to the top of this precipitous rock.

Paranavitana is of the opinion that a festival similar to the *Giragga Samajja* of ancient India may have been held at Sigiriya.

Lord Agboyi (c. 9th Century) wrote:

4. [නැ]ගි අලුයම අවුජ් බලය් සිටියිනි මෙහි මය්
වින්දිමි මඳමරු ගස එත තමු(රු)වෙනෙහි සුවඳ් (මෙහි)

[Nä]gi aluyama avuj balay siṭiyini mehi may
Vindimi manda-maru gasa eta tamu(ru)-venehi suvand (mehi)

As I, having climbed (up), came here at dawn and to stood looking at (this), I enjoy the fragrance of the clusters of lotuses as the gentle breeze comes blowing here.

Poet Dev came at high noon and looked at the sun to discern whether it was time for his meal, and abruptly saw the damsels nearby.

356. ජීවෙල් ගෙන යින් මෙ සිරිබර්නි මයි ආ රස
බැලුමො ගුයුන බ[ල]ත් බෙ[ය*]න්‍දිහි රන්වනුන් දුටිමො

Jivel gen=ayin me siri-barni mayi ā rasa
Bälumo guyuna ba[la] t be[ya*]nd'hi ran-vanun duṭmo

As I came (here) bringing (with me) means of sustenance, delight came (into being) from the abundant splendour of this. We looked at the sky and, when we looked, we saw the golden- coloured ones on the mountain side.

Agboyi, the evening visitor saw the damsels and compared them to the flower of the blue *katarolu* and that of the (golden) fence gourd, *vatakolu.*

334. නිල්ක[ට]රොළ මලෙකැ ඇවුණු වැටිකොළ මල සෙය්
සැඳැගැ සිහි වෙන්නෙය් මහනෙල්වන [හ]ය් රන්වන හුන්

Nil-ka[ṭ]roḷa malekä ävuṇu väṭkoḷa mala sey
Sändägä sihi venne-y mahanel-vana [ha]y ran-vana hun

*Like a vatkola flower entangled in a blue katorola flower, the golden-coloured one who stood together with the lily-coloured one will be remembered at the advent of the even*ing.

Those who ascended Sigiriya and recorded what they saw of the scenic beauty, the frescoes, or any other aspects have indeed left us an invaluable treasure. They made it possible for us to inherit a little of their wisdom, their sense of aesthetics and their emotional life – gifts far more valuable than any artifacts such as implements, coins and ornaments!

We do not know for certain who the Sigiriya artists were. The manner in which they were tutored and the influences that had a bearing on their work can only be conjectured. But what doubt is there about the heritage that has been left to us by poets? Their records testify to their being our own ancestors who came from various regions of our own Island. For instance, Sangapal who "established the pleasaunce Palavatu-vela" wrote.

17. (ප)ලාව(තු)වෙ[ලැ] අරමබ් තැනූ සඟපල්(බතී)මි මෙ ගිය ලීමි
බෙයන්‍ද් ගොසින් බැලූමො සිත් සුරුැස්නා සෙය්
බණතුජ් නොබෙණෙනන් ඇ[සිපි]යෙව් එයුන් ලයු නැත්තේ

(Pa)lāva(tu)-ve[lä] aramb tänū Saṅgapal-(batī)mi me giya līmi
Beyand gosin bälūmo sit surusnā sey
Baṇat=uj no-beṇenan ä[si-pi]yev eyun luyu nätte

We went to the mountainside and, in such manner as the mind becomes well pleased, looked at these (i.e. the women) who do not speak even when (we) speak (to them). Of them, indeed, there is not (even) the falling of eyelids.

Poet Tilimala of Ruhuna wrote:

123. රුහුණින්ආ [ති]ළි[මල] ගී
ගැහැනී ලියන් බෙයන්ඳ්හි රන්වනුන් අතුරෙ
මන ම තමහට් මෙ ගත් දිගැස්නි කුම් කොට් සහන්නෙ[මි]
තිළිමල ගී

Ruhuṇin ā [Ti]ḷi[mala] gī
Gähänī liyan beyand'hi ran-vanun ature
Mana ma tamahaṭ me gat digäsni kum koṭ sahanne[mi]
Tiḷimala gī

The slender women, among the golden-coloured ones on the mountain side, took my mind solely to themselves. O long-eyed one, what may I do to sustain myself?

and Jet Mala of Polonnaruva wrote this verse;

233. පොලොනරුයෙන් ආ ජේ(ට්ම)ලමි මෙ ගී ලීමි
ලිය මල් [කැ]නක් ග[ත්] දිලි අත්නි [ලො]බනා සෙයි
ගත් මන මය් දිගැස් බෙයදහි සම්වන ක් ද යෙහෙ

Polonaruyen ā Je(ṭ-ma)lami me gī līmi
Liya mal-[kä]nak ga[t] dil[i] atni [lo]banā seyi
Gat mana may digäs beyadahi samvana k da yehe

The long-eyed (slender) woman who, in her radiant hand, has taken a cluster of flowers in an enticing manner, has captivated my heart'. 'Is it a dark-complexioned one on the mountain side that is good (for you)?'

Sanga of Ruhuna's Pandulagama inscribed the lines:

279. රුහුණ් පඬුලගමු සඟ මෙ [ගී]
බෙණෙත සැනැ නැතතන් ජො[ලො] එය මැසි තු[බු]යුනට
නො[තු]බුයුහට නො [මෙ එ]ය යන් එ රන්[වනුන්] ජැහැ

Ruhuṇ -Paṇḍulagamu Saṅga me [gī]
Beṇ eta sänä nättan jo[lo] eya mäsi tu[bu]yunaṭa
No-[tu]buyuhaṭa no [me e]ya yan e ran-[vanun] jähä

When those who do not have love speak, the burning (of the heart) might come (into being) to those possessed of anger. This may not come to those who do not possess (anger). Go (away, therefore), discarding these golden-coloured ones.

and from Mihidal of Sanladkubura this epigram:

441. ශ්‍රී මි[හිද]ල්මි සන්ලද්[කුබු]රෙන් [මෙහි ආ] දවැසැ [ලීමි]
ලැබු මෙ සි වී නො මඳ් හි [ම බු]න් බලත ඇති වන්
මන මෙන් බෙ(යඳ් මෙ නැගී) අව රන්(වනුන් අතුරෙ)

Srī Mi[hida]lmi San-lad-[kubu]ren [mehi ā] daväsä [līmi]
Läbu me si vī no mand hi[mabu]n balata äti van
Mana men be(yand me nägī) ava ran(vanun ature)

When, having ascended this mountain side in accordance with my mind, I am come in the midst of the golden-coloured ones, is not this smile, received when looking at the ladies as they are, enough?

While Agbo of Dunuvagam wrote:

514. සිටිත් ගල්මතමබුරෙ දිගැසින් තොල් මොළොක් කොට්
කිපී රජ සි[ටි] තම වෙත කිපී කි වජන් නො එ මෙට
(දුනුවාග)මු අ[ග්]බො[මි]

Siṭit gal-mat=ambure digäsin tol moḷok koṭ
Kipī raja si[ṭi] tama veta kipī ki vajan no e meṭa
(Dunuvāga)mu A[g]bo[mi]

The king remains enraged at us; the word which (he) said in being enraged will not come to this'. (So thinking, as it were), the long-eyed ones, having made their lips tender, stand in the sky on the summit of the rock.

Our classical literary works were written on talipot palm leaves, and as they were transcribed from time to time, several changes in the texts resulted. It is possible that we would never have a chance of seeing the original manuscripts. Not so, in the case of the Sigiriya lyrics. We are able to see and read the very handwriting of the pre-10th century poets even today; and as such, the graffiti are a national treasure of no mean worth. It is fitting that we go to the very environment of the frescoes at Sigiriya to appreciate their beauty. Can we enjoy genuine pleasure by looking at a model or a photograph? But nothing prevents a person who has never seen the Mirror Wall from grasping the meaning of these verses and appreciating their contents aesthetically. Enshrined in the verses is beauty unseen in frescoes, even though the frescoes inspired the literary compositions. That, is something we should never forget.

The Sigiriya verses are like a doorway through which one may observe the culture, feelings, thoughts, aspirations, customs and manners, settlements, names and titles, of the people of the time; equally important is the knowledge we get of the contemporary language. Though there is a mutual relationship between the frescoes and the lyrics, the former is like a silent "movie" while the latter is comparable to a "talkie" that portrays live cross-sections of the society of those times.

We are fortunate to possess this unique heritage which reflects various aspects of the life of successive periods of time. Some of the poets who ascended Sigiriya saw the frescoes and experienced the beauty of the surroundings and of the totality of the environment of the Rock and expressed themselves by scribbling verses on the Wall. The compositions themselves testify that they were executed with a sense of responsibility.

Budal refrained from composing a verse precisely because many of those who had experienced the beauty of the place had done so:

'බුදල්මි
සියො වැ ආමි.
සිහිගිරි බැලිමි.
බැලු බැලු බොහො ජනා ගී ලීයෙන් නොලීමි.'

Another thought it his duty and responsibility to compose a song in order to pay off the debt of having experienced the glory of the environment:

405. මෙයට් ඇවිජ් ගියක් නො බදහ යි නගින බියෙන්
බියපතිමි [තැ]වෙයි හද අව රනවනන් අතරෙ

Meyaṭ ävij giyak no bada-ha yi nagina biyen
Biya-patimi [tä]veyi hada ava rana-vanan atare

I am apprehensive with the fear arising from (the thought): 'He has not been able to compose a stanza (even) after having come here.' My heart becomes tormented when (I am) come to the midst of the golden-coloured ones.

The poet, in the midst of the golden coloured ones is apparently excited, and finds it difficult to compose himself, and the verse is written to allay any fear of his being found guilty of ingratitude. For those who tried hard to break the silence of the damsels in the romantic environment the only way open was poetry. Would not an aesthete who had ascended the rock and won the heart of a damsel through his poetic ability be further encouraged by the sight of the inscribed verses? The following verse by Nand from Ruhuna appears to have been expressed as a result of such an experience:

125. බලන් මෙ [දි]ග්නෙත් නො කියන් ගී [හැ]ජෙ [ත වෙ]ත
කුමට් ජු හු තොමො තුබු ළ මෙහි අ බලනුයුන් දග
රුහුණින් ආ නඳ[මි]

Balan me [di]g-net no kiyan gī [hä]je [ta ve]ta
Kumaṭ ju hū tomo tubu ḷa mehi a balanuyun daga
Ruhuṇin ā Nand[mi]

Look (if you please) at this long-eyed one, but do not recite songs, (for) she would then be drawn to you. Wherefore did she, who had a heart, bind in fetters those who are come here and look at her?.

126. [නු]යුන් මන බඳ්නා පියවුරු බැලුම්රුස්නා
අ බෙයදහි රන්වන් මන මතහස් යො මු කළ තමා

[Nu]yun mana badnā piyavuru bälum-rusnā
A beyadahi ranvan mana mata-has yo mu kaḷa tamā

Ah! The golden-coloured one on the mountain side, who entices one's eye and mind and whose breasts are delightful to look at, directed my mind to the intoxicated swans.

If not for the testimony of these lyrics it is difficult to imagine that the society of the times appreciated poetry so deeply. These lyrics are evidence of the common folks' love of poetry.

169. ජහග මෙ සිතිවිලි අන් කුම් කියන්නෙය් ගියක්
බද් මා නෑ බදනෙ [ස]ග්[ඉ]සිරැ නැග ගන් සිහිගිරි

Jahaga me sitivili an kum kiyanney giyak
Bad mā nä badane [sa]g-[i]sirä näga gan Sihigiri

Abandon these (melancholy) thoughts. What else is there to be said by me who composed a verse? The splendour of heaven does not hold me. Ascend Sihigiri thyself.

The damsel here is sorrowful over a misunderstanding about her lover, the poet, and no words of love can appease her. "Shed your sorrow. I have composed the song, what more am I to say?", he seems to say. Nothing seems to be beyond the possibility of a song.

If one composes a song it was possible that a damsel would be attracted to him, as evidenced by the composition of Nand who came from Ruhuna referred to above.

A poet seems to say to a damsel, "it looks as though you have no attachment to songs these days", and discovers too late that he should not have said so. Non-attachment to songs is suggestive of the absence of intelligence and perspicacity. Repenting, he declares "I said so in fun", and tries to comfort her.

369. කී යමො මෙදවස් ත ගී ලැසි නො යි කෙළි මා
කෙ එත් තොප කෙරෙ වී එඩි එත් උනට් අක්මය්(වය්)

Kī yamo me-davas ta gī läsi no yi keḷi mā
Ke et topa kere vī eḍi et unaṭ akmay(vay)

It is (in) fun that it has been said by me: 'We shall go away, songs are not wished for by you today.' Who will come having become arrogant towards you?. If (such) do come, may you forgive them.

Another poet called Mahavit Siv addressed a poem of immortal worth to a damsel who, on being pleased by it, tarried on the Sigiriya terrace:

209. තනරනමලී ලී (ග)තින් (අ)මය එක් වන ගී
සිටි ගත නිල මෙ බෙයදිහි තු[ට ළ වූ]බව අශ්වය

Tana-rana-malī lī (ga)tin (a)maya ek vana gī
Siṭi gata nili me beyadihi tu[ṭa ḷa vū] bava a(ṅ)gvaya

The damsel (who wears) a golden chain on her breast, as (she) accepted the song which is like nectar, took her stand on this mountain side, having made it her abode, giving expression to the fact that (her) heart has become rejoiced.

She does not leave the rock terrace because she does not like to leave behind the songs.

The composition of Mihind portrays how even one tormented by the worst grief can be comforted by a song:

472. නො ලබන්නෙ බසක් ගි[ය] බඳිමි හො සෙර සෙ සිවි
ම යත් යත් අය්හ නො වි ද බ[ලමි] න් සොවින් හිඳිනා

No labanne basak gi[ya] bandmi ho sera se sivi
Ma yat yat ayha no vi da ba[lami] n sovin hindinā

Receiving no word (from her), I composed this song. She smiled in the manner of a roguish woman – (she) who remains (there), whenever I pass (that way), gazing (forward as if) in grief, though (in fact) she was not unhappy.

The poet approached the damsel who does not speak a word. Although it would have been proper to ignore such a female, the poet thinks it appropriate to compose a poem despite the fact that her reaction is silence.

Soon she shed her sorrow and, as he walked away, cast him a smile coquettishly . Such is the power of a poem; and the damsel, silent in sorrow at first, becomes light of heart soon after reading it.

These, certainly, are not mere stray thoughts of poets. Writers react emotionally to contemporary social conventions and values. Among them too, poets stand above the rest. Hence it is justifiable to arrive at conclusions regarding contemporary popular attitudes based on the evidence supplied by these poets.

Many are the compositions that help us to discern the high standard of poetics and the level of literary appreciation of the common people during the centuries when the Sigiriya verses were being composed. All of them are not considered here. The poem by Sivala Bata of Venavana is a case in point:

556. වෙණවාණවැසි සිවලබතිමි බල බ[ද ගී]
බලනනට රමණී අහස පොකුණ කැටැබිති
ගෙහිනුහු සිතතම ගීරස පූ කෙ[නක] මෙන් නො

Veṇavāṇa-väsi Sivala-batimi bala ba[da gī]
Balananaṭa ramaṇī ahasa pokuṇa käṭä-biti
Gehinuhu sitatama gī-rasa pū ke[naka] men no

The sky, the pond and the mirror wall are delightful to look at. Are not the women in the painting like those who have drunk the nectar of songs?

What did the poet intend to convey to us?

When you look at the Sky Pond from the top of the Sigiri summit it appears as if the mirror wall is reflected in the pond. The mirror wall with quiet contemplation is an object of meditation. The damsels are devoid of speech and physical movement. They therefore appear as though in motionless contemplation inspired by the lyrics.

The idea expressed by him echoes the meaning of *Vedyantara sparsa sunyo* of the *Sahitya* Darpana, viz., "In poetic appreciation (one's) mind is attached to a single point without being tainted by the touch of any distraction". It reflects the high standard of literary appreciation on the part of these poets. The ladies represented in these frescoes apparently have come to life through a deep and unprecedented awareness and experience of life and the outlook on life of these poets, through the form of poetry adopted by them. It looks as though the Sigiriya damsels, intoxicated and drunk with the aesthetic stimulation of the songs, thrive on the strength and the mutual attraction between the frescoes in the gallery and the verses on the Mirror Wall. This symbiotic relationship of the two inspires the visitors to derive the highest aesthetic delight.

THE COQUETTISH SMILE, THE SEEDS OF THE MELON

The word *Sahṛda* in the terminology of literary criticism and appreciation has the meaning of a person endowed with the sense of aesthetic taste or sentiment (*rasa*). A *Sahṛda* is a person having a heart similar to that of the poet. He possesses a friendly disposition. Aesthetic taste is brought about by emotional interaction between the creator and the person who enjoys the creation.

The *Sahṛda* too is a *rasika*, one who appreciates. Often enough the artist is also a *rasika*. The artist, certainly is endowed with a sense of taste, at least in so far as his field of art is concerned. The creator of a work of art and the *rasika* should have a mutual friendship and a cordial understanding. The unity of feeling, the friendship brought into being between the artist who creates an original work and the *rasika* can be compared to the supreme bliss of communion between two lovers. It is an experience of mutual identification. Enjoyment of art amounts to a communion between two sahṛdas. To the degree that the heart – the mirror of the *rasika* - is polished and clean, the experience of the artist is reflected in the heart-mirror of the *rasika*.

Treasures of *rasa* accumulated over thousands of years and inherited by us are innumerable. Any work of art that does not commune with persons with aesthetic taste remains just a physical object. In the minds of those who are attuned to *rasa* are stored all the requisites of *rasa*. Yet, instances of *rasa* being generated and blossoming and bearing fruit are indeed rare.

We have accumulated a wealth of experience over the cycles of birth and death, depending on our deeds, both good and bad. We bring with us a balance sheet in which is recorded all the credits and debits. At the termination of a life, on the death bed, when one is about to start a new life, only powerful experiences will be recollected. They are so powerful as to accompany a person to the next birth.

The reflections of these experiences that are accumulated and accompany our lives are stored in the form of a powerful force. This force is called *vasana* (sensibility). It is a force, a quality, a maturity of the mind. The strength of the sensibility depends on the subtle sense of aesthetic taste. It is due to the strength of this sensibility that the aesthetic feelings bear fruit in the process of enjoyment of art. The dormant feelings in the mind of a *rasika* will blossom and bear fruit giving rise to new feelings.

Sigiriya is different from the huge cave complexes of Ajanta, Dunhuang, and other sites that contain paintings. At Sigiriya, there is in addition a mirror-wall. Inscribed on it and preserved are the impressions and feelings of poets whose minds were stimulated by the portraits of the Sigiri damsels. Sigiri poetry remains a befitting reward to the talent of the artists who painted the damsels. It is our endeavour in this chapter to discuss a single poem, describing the damsels, selected out of a large corpus, inscribed on the mirror wall. This is a rhymed quatrain in the *Yon-mat-vala* metre.

103. කොමුළ් අමඩ්ලෙඩ් ලින සී
එ බොඳ මියුර් යහ බැසී
එ කපල්දල වන් දිගැසී
මන ජල්(ව)යි (සිත්) නො මුසී

Komuḷ amaḍ-leḍ lina sī
E bonda miyur yaha bäsī
E kapal-dala van digäsī
Mana jal(va)yi (sit) no musī

(She), The coquettish smile given by whom is (comparable to the rows of) seeds of the melon, Her pleasant speech is as sweet as the

marrow of that (fruit), whose long eye is (like) a segment of the rind of the same (fruit), inflames my heart and leaves not my mind.

The smile of the Sigiri damsel with open lips, displaying her teeth, is reminiscent of the rows of seeds of the melon, well set inside the fruit. The pleasant speech of the long-eyed one is cool and sweet as the marrow of the melon. The long eyes of the damsel are like segments of the outer rind of the same fruit. Her teeth, sweet words and eyes are reminiscent of the melon in one respect or another. Thus, at a glance, the Sigiri damsel resembles the inside of the melon in all respects. Yet, this likeness is only on the outside. What would it be like after partaking of this melon and tasting it?

The melon is a fruit that cools the body. It dispels heat too. The very thoughts of the melon bring about a sense of coolness. On the other hand, thoughts about the damsels usually arouse the heat of passion. They arouse a feeling of heat or fire. The mind is kindled. It starts burning through lust. It torments the mind. There is, thus, no peace. In a way, though cooling, this is the nature of the melon too. In certain other respects, Sigiri damsels are different. This poem, written by a poet whose heart is set ablaze by their beauty, attracts our mind like the coolness of the melon.

What then is the experience behind this Sigiri poem? How does it affect our minds? The teeth, eyes, pleasant speech, all these had brought to the poet's mind the image of the melon not a real melon, but an imaginary one. It was in the poet's thoughts that the seeds of the melon, its shape etc., had taken a special form. The similarity between the melon, on the one hand, and the beauty and the lovely form of the damsels, on the other, had been perceived in the imagination of the poet.

Bringing about *rasa* is, thus, a process of inter-communication based on the thoughts of the creative artist and the person who enjoys the aesthetic taste. The creative power of the artist and the ability of the *rasika* to experience the art have been increased manifold by sensibility (*vasana*), a quality which gets accumulated through the process of recollection over many lives.

The word *rasika* which has been translated here, as a person of taste and elsewhere as a sensitive soul has no satisfactory equivalent in English. The word "person of taste" is more or less a literal translation of the term which takes into consideration the term *rasa* in a limited sense. Rasa as sentiment is elaborated in Sanskrit poetics to consist of *Navarasa* and *rasika* is a person with the gift to discern and distinguish them. Of the many translations of this term *rasa,* taste is but one. This *rasika* also means a person of cultivated taste. The difficulty of giving a satisfactory translation of the word *rasika* derives from the fact that there is no equivalent English term to render the comprehensive meaning of *rasa* in Sanskrit poetics. The term connoisseur sometimes used by writers in English is far from adequate as it connotes the cognitive rather than the affective aspect of *rasika.* For the reasons stated above, some writers prefer to retain the term *rasika* as a technical term in their writings. The renderings given here are in keeping with the context in which they have been used and are aimed at giving simple, non technical descriptions.

Pleasant is the coolness of the melon. The coolness is felt only when one eats it. Could it not be that a lesson learnt through experience in life is echoed here in the poem? What is seen as similar externally is internally very different. Tormented by the fire of lust, as a result of making love to a Sigiri damsel on the false assumption that she possessed coolness, the elegantly inscribed words on the mirror-wall are not second to the painting drawn on the mountain side.

The damsel portrayed in the mind of the painter has been depicted on the mountain side. Similarly, the beauty of the damsel that stirred the poet and the gracefulness of the paintings are reflected in the poem inscribed on the mirror-wall. The Sigiri painter, of course, did not have the opportunity to read the poems on the mirror-wall. On the contrary the opportunities afforded to the *rasika* to experience and enjoy the paintings as well as the poetry that blossomed on the imagination of the poet are numerous. It is, thus, left to the *rasika* to experience the beauty in its entirety, depending on his own sensibility.

THE CHARM OF SIGIRI POETRY: REFLECTIONS ON THE MIND

The mind, intangible and unseen! How else can one know about it other than by thought which itself is an act of the mind? Yet, true indeed are the words of Bhikkhu Dharmasena who tried to explain to us the real nature of the mind.

> **This mind is verily so fickle, unsteady like a wind-blown kite. It is fitful, because it does not stay fixed on one objective, just like a small child who is unable to stay still. (*Saddharmaratnavaliya*, 13th cen.)**

Poetry is the unique outcome of fixing that very intractable mind on one objective, even for a moment. The paintings, adding life to the lifeless rock surface of Sigiri, and the verses, scribbled with a *panhinda* on the mirror wall are but the elegant trains of thought that welled up in the minds of the painters and the poets of Sigiri.

Visitors thought of coming on a pleasure trip to see the damsels of Sigiri. When they arrive at Sigiriya they are enthralled by the beauty of

these damsels. Many a change would occur in their minds, just by having a glimpse of those enchanting figures on the rock surface. The poets sometimes are moved even to concentrate on the mind itself.

The fascination of the sound that floats into the ear, the fragrance of the smell that titillates the nose, the charm of the figure that enchants the eye, the exquisiteness of the caress that is felt by the body, all depend on the nuances of the mind. Why a thousand different souls feel about a thousand things in hundred thousand ways has to do with the variable nature of the mind. The mind can take on many and varying dimensions depending on place and time. This is how the nature of the mind was perceived by a poet of Sigiri:

77. තමහට නො දිස් වූ මෙන් වෙ (ද) සිත ජනෙන (තම)
දිසෙයි නැගෙන බඳු සිකි (අ)බුරෙහි කිමිඳි සෙ තහට

Tamahaṭa no dis vū men ve (da) sita janne (tama)
Diseyi nägena bandu siki (a)burehi kimindi se tahaṭa

Is it not in the manner that (a thing) has appeared to one's self that one's mind cognizes (it)? What (appears to me) like rising up appears to you, (my) friend, as if it has dived in the sky?

Whereas another poet had seen the ladies as if they were half immersed in the sky pond, this poet sees them as emerging from the pond. The figures depict the ladies only above their waists and so one can visualize them as suspended on or either rising from or descending into clouds. What one's mind conceives the same the eye sees! On the other hand an object that evokes sorrow in one person might appear immensely pleasurable to another. The mind can take on varied forms at different times. Thus, if one can control one's mind, it would be like taking control of everything else. How many of us who strive hard to possess a comfortable vehicle can enjoy the comfort of a public vehicle which offers the same amenities? Why can't we enjoy a public park and enjoy fully its pleasures, in the same way as we would enjoy a privately owned one? Is it because we are slaves to the craving to possess it exclusively for ourselves?

The desire to possess the beautiful and the valued exclusively will always be there, as long as there is desire. This realization evoked a profound response from poet Kitala hailing from Ruhuna:

34. වනවූ හිමින් හිමබි යැ යි හෙ සිතිය තමා
වි යහපත් දෙතා බෙයදහි රන්වනුන් දුටු යෙන්

Vana-vū -himin himabi yä yi he sitiya tamā
Vi yahapat detā beyadahi ranvanun duṭu yen

He, when he thought that those who are separated from their lord were his ladies, became doubly happy as he saw the golden-coloured ones on the mountain side.

If someone were to suppose that the pangs of separation suffered were his own and that they were weeping for his sake, his attachment to them would indeed be doubled.

If the feeling of personal entity cannot be eradicated, one can spread that possessive feeling all around. Why cannot we therefore let that possessive feeling embrace everybody so that there will be no difference between us and others – even our enemies? That seems to be the philosophy of the poet. The ladies of Sigiri are one's own. Their grief too becomes one's own grief, and their beauty too. If one could create this sense of universal consciousness, one would feel a tremendous sense of joy. Sarvam buddhimayam.

180. ඇවිද් සුවෙ [ල]ද අප සිහිගිරි (කතුන්) අතුරෙහි
සිකි සඳ තමන් බල නැ[ගැ]සිහි තමහට (වෙ) එහි ඇති
නොවි සිහි යන්නමහ මහවන් හෙළිල්ල[බි]යැන්
නො හිඳූ යැ(ත) මෙ තැනින සෙද ම ම න සිටිය නො වන්නෙන්

Ävid suve [la]da apa Sihigiri (katun) aturehi
Siki -sanda taman bala nä[gä] sihi tamahaṭa (ve) ehi äti
No-vi sihi yannamaha mahavan heḷilla[bi]yän
No hindä yä(ta) me -tänina seda ma ma na siṭiya no-vannen

Having come to Sihagiri, happiness has been obtained by us in the midst of the lovely women. O esteemed friend, climb up and see (for) yourself; what is there will (then) be remembered by you.

Forgive (me), O fair damsels. I go away without remembering (you), for, as I, without tarrying, go away hastily from this place, my mind does not remain (here).

The poet says that, when one is among the damsels of Sigiri, one feels exalted because one's mind is full of their presence. How very true! After all, what is pleasure? Is it a feeling or an event? Or is it the change in one's mind which occurs when one considers what has happened?

Of our experiences, which ones are unpleasant? When one thinks back, do not even the past disagreeable experiences bring about pleasant feelings? Do endured hardships, when pondered upon later, create the same discomfort? Does a person who has recovered from an illness undergo the same pain when he looks back on those days of misery? Indeed, there is a certain pleasure in looking back on those unpleasant days. Thus we see that pleasure is found in the happy thoughts arising in the mind when one ponders on a past experience. Hence how fortunate it is if one can experience again something which was so wonderful as to have remained fixed in one's mind?

Cumaratunga Munidasa says in his magnificent poem *Piya Samara:* "Guilt is what one has to repent when one looks back on a past event."

Those indeed are the very sentiments expressed by the poet of Sigiri who wrote verse 180.

Why do these ladies appear to us as lovers? We cannot say for certain. May be it is just a predetermined idea. Let us take another example. Why do we love life? We cannot say for certain. Isn't it just habit?

82. මෙ අග්නන් (නු)ගි වැ පැනෙන්නෙක් පුරුද්දෙන් සි(ති)
මෙ දිවියට් රිසි මෙන් රිසි වනෙනක් සිහිගිරි

Me agnan (nu)gi vä pänennek purudden si(ti)
Me diviyaṭ risi men risi vannek Sihigirī

One to whom these women appear as fit for company thought (so) by (force of) habit.One to whom Sihigiri is desirable (thought so) in the same manner as his desire for life.

In this boundless *Samsara,* the person who has always been with one, in pleasure and pain, is one's beloved wife. These damsels too appear like her. And the love for Sigiri, the abode of those beloved damsels, is as dear as one's love for life itself.

The poet Kiti who arrived at Sigiri raises a fascinating question. He realized the potency of love only after returning home. Everyone else had fallen asleep. "She stayed beside the rock to brush aside the sorrow in my heart. There is no doubt about that. But oh! Why does she linger in front of my eye when I am trying to sleep?"

32. කිති මුගලන මලන ගෙ කිති (මි ලීමි)
ම සොව නිව ඇ මෙසෙයි දුදුළ සෙල අඩදරිහි
විසිය යහඅසරට නු කිම නිඳැ නො ගිය යහනෙයි

Kiti Mugalana Malana ge Kiti (mi līmi)
Ma sova niva ä meseyi d[u]d[u]ḷa-sela aḍadarihi
Visiya yaha-asaraṭa nu kima ninda no giya yahaneyi

(It is) indeed for happy companionship that she, having assuaged my grief, dwelt in this manner at the edge of the fortress rock. (But) why did (I) not go to sleep in (my) bed?

How many among us venture to lay bare the true feelings that arise in our hearts? In a world where people think something, say something else and do something quite different, it would certainly be extraordinary if someone were to give expression to a thought in the same form as it arose in his mind.

69. මෙසා තොප බඳුහු කියවූහ සිතන්නා සෙ
ඔක(ඩ)නා සියලඟ් ලොමුදහ ගැනවී සිහිගි(රී)

Mesā topa banduhu kiyavūha sitannā se
Oka(ḍ)nā siyalaṅg lom=udaha gänavī Sihigi(rī)

(Persons) like you have made so many (people) speak just as they think. (By you) has (also) been caused, at Sihigiri, the bristling of the hair which thrills the whole body.

Ladies, who send pleasurable sensations right through the body and make one's hair stand on end, there indeed is no possibility of covering up the sensuous feelings about you which well up in our minds when we are in your presence.

In examining Sigiri poetry we realize that these are nothing but delightful expressions of genuine feeling. These ladies incite those who come before them to utter unabashedly the real feelings that well up in their hearts. Isn't it proof of the power they wield? Genuine love and truthfulness go hand in hand. They are inseparable.

Poet Mugalan from Ruhuna who observed the life-like quality of these paintings pays the highest possible tribute to the unknown painter:

161. වන යි මෙ සිතුවර් තබය අයිමි අජහස්
අවන් කො ජ මෙය නො ජන්නො බෙයඳැහි රන වනුන අතුරෙ

Vana yi me situvar tabaya ayimi ajahas
Avan ko ja meya no janno beyandahi rana-vanuna ature

Lest this painter depict (them), I came here having kept (behind my) thoughts. Where are those who do not know this among (the people) who are coming to the midst of the golden-coloured ones on the mountain side.

This painter who has done such wonders with his brush, creating such life-like images is surely capable of portraying even the very thoughts in the minds of people. Therefore the poet in fear left his thoughts at home. The capacity of the painter to portray not only the visible, but even the invisible thoughts was no secret to the damsels of Sigiri as well as to those who came to see them. Poet Mugalan seems to have decided to take precautions after he saw the golden coloured damsels and noted the sentiments expressed by the many admirers who visited them.

Some poets are deep thinkers. The Buddha himself has recognized a category called *chinta kavi* as we note in the *Anguttara Nikaya*. The poet who wrote verse No. 191 has an opinion to express about those thinkers:

191. සිතන්නො ජු වෙත් සිරිබර්නි මඳ්ගන්නායූ
තොප නුයුන් මානෙල් සඟළ හය් සරි කළයුන්

Sitanno ju vet siri-barni mand-gannāyu
Topa nuyun mānel -saṅgaḷa hay sari-kaḷayun

Those who compare your eyes with the pair of blue lilies are thinkers (indeed) - but (they) are (persons) who take little out of the abundance of (your) splendour.

How many would have compared the eyes of these ladies to blue water-lilies, before the Sigiri Graffiti and after.

TO LEAP FROM A PEAK

**My death will not occur
Until she grants her order.
But my life I cannot support,
For fear that she may not accord
A worthy place or room
In her love, to Cupid's doom.
Alas! My love a fairy queen
Is in a quandary embodied, I mean.
Towards her yea! turns my mind
And sure, soon would she me bind.
Both internally and externally,
So that I may not move freely.**

Verse 23 in Paranavitana's "Sigiri Graffiti" states that:

23. නො ජ මරණ තොමො (අ)න දි නො මරනා (ෙ)තක්නි
ජීවි නහෙයි තොමො නු(රා) මා (යෙ)වෙන බියෙනි
ඇතුළතිනි ජු බැහැරියෙන් එකවට ගත[නි]
අබු මිනිසුන් ඉසිලු කු(ළ) පිනූ සෙයිනි

No ja maraṇa tomo (a)na di no maranā t(e)kni
Jivi na-heyi tomo nu(rā) ma (ye)vena biyeni
Ätuḷatini ju bähäriyen eka-vaṭa gata[ni]
Abu minisun isilu ku(ḷa) pinū seyini

There is no death until (she) herself gives the order and kills (me). Life also is impossible on account of the fear of my being banished from her affection. As one is captivated at once internally as well as externally, the supporting of women by men is like leaping from a peak.

A poet visiting Sigiri falls in love with a nymph painted in a grotto. He communicates his feelings to her. The plaintive poetic conception contains inter alia a touch of witty satire.

I am not destined to die until you terminate my life. I fear death lest your love will not be for me. I am in a quandary.

The life of lovers subject to torment, internally and externally, with no room either to live or die, is as problematic as a leap from a peak.

If she so orders, the poet is ready to face death. The moment he thinks that she may not love him, he gets disgusted with life. Thus the poet suffers from within and without, but with a true realization of the nature of women. What consolation could there be for a mortal ensnared by the guile of a woman? It is like unto a leap from a peak. After the leap the individual would realize his folly; he can neither go back to his former position, nor can he remain where he is fallen, for he would soon die.

The beauties are on the edge of the precipice. The poets imagine them leaping from the peak, being unable to bear the torment of separation from their lovers. The poets repeatedly mention that the beauties are leaping from the peak.

300. නරනිඳ් ලයු මෙළෙයින් සෙවින් ළ නො වහන්නෙන්
බෙයඳ්හි රන්වනු ගිරි හිස්ති හෙන් නයුන් වැන්නො

Naranind layu meḷeyin sevin ḷa no vahannen
Beyand'hi ran-vanu giri -hisni hen nayun vänno

The golden-coloured ones on the mountain side have the appearance of those hurling themselves down from the summit of the rock, their hearts being not able to bear (themselves) up because of grief, since the King, indeed, is dead.

The damsels of golden colour living on the mountain side <u>sans parail</u> appear to leap from the peak with sorrow.

499. බලම්හ යි සිටි ගිරිබිත්හි දිග්නෙත් කි [වෙ] මා
බෙයඳ්හි රන්වනු ගිරිබිත්නි හෙන්නයුන් වැන්නො

Balamha yi siṭi giri-bit'hi dig-net ki [v]e mā
Beyand'hi ran-vanu giri-bitni hennayun vänno

The long-eyed one stands on the rock wall, thinking 'We shall look at (him)'. But it has been said by me that the golden-coloured ones on the mountain side have the appearance of those hurling (themselves) down from the rock wall.

As their lover, the king, is no more, the long-eyed ones on the rock wall yearn to see him "who is above all." Alas! he is no more, so they appear to leap from the peak, because of their great grief. These two verses have similarities, but they differ widely as poetic creations.

Verse No. 300 mentioned above says that the beauties appear to leap from the peak owing to the unbearable grief caused by the death of the King.

The long-eyed ones were there on the wall gazing at the poet. But the poet as an artist imagines them to be in the process of leaping from the peak.

The beauties are no doubt widows. They could not wait till the poet approached them. They come to the edge of the precipice and await his arrival. All that, is no secret to the poet. He understands that, but he would not imply or express it. The widows should not behave like this; therefore in order to maintain their dignity the poet tells a white lie – that is – "Oh they appear to leap from the peak" (through their great grief for their dear departed one – the king).

The lines of Utura Abu Sivikala, a poetess, and those of Budal, a poet have both linguistic and semantic similarities. They both imagine (a) that the damsels are hurling themselves down from the rock and (b) that they are "leaping from the peak" respectively.

It was the external beauty, the feminine appearance and love of the nymphs that, in fact, attracted a majority of the poets. If ever they referred to their psychology it was only their love that they spoke of. But a poet called Mihindal Bata has viewed these damsels differently and thus praised them for their courage and resoluteness. He says:

653. බලත් මට රිසි වියි මොයුන් සිත් [දැ]ඩි වී ඇති
ගිරිබිත්හි රන්වනු ගිරිහිසිනි [හෙ]න්නයුන් වැන්නො

Balat maṭ risi viyi moyun sit [dä]ḍi vī äti
Giri-bit'hi ran-vanu giri-hisini [he]nnayun vänno

When looking at (them), these damsels, having minds become resolute, became desirable for me. The golden-coloured ones on the rock wall have the appearance of those hurling themselves (down) from the summit of the rock.

"I looked at them, they attracted my mind for they are resolute, determined and bold. The golden-coloured ones appear to leap from the mountain peak, through their great grief".

It is observed by Paranavitana that the boldness attributed to the nymphs is in keeping with the poetic imagination that they are ready to leap from the peak. The central conception of the poets is that the Sigiri damsels are going to leap from the peak.

The author of the verse No. 131 expresses a different opinion. He believes that the damsels, who are ever ready to die for the sake of their lover are worthy of honour and respect. The poet seems to have had great love for moral values.

131. වැටි මියත් පියහට් ඇඳි වැන්නී ගල්හී
යහමඟයනන් සස ලෙස ලෙණැසි නෙ වැ න්දිය කා නම්

Väṭi miyat piyahaṭ ändi vännī galhī
Yaha-maṅga-yanan sasa lesa leṇäsi ne vä ndiya kā nam

Like Truth by those treading the path of goodness, by whom, indeed, was the gazelle-eyed one not honoured – she who is like one painted on the rock whilst hurling herself down and dying for the sake of(her) lover.

"The gazelle-eyed one resembles a maiden painted on the rock wall while letting herself fall from the peak through despair, for her lover is no more. By whom should she not be honoured as truth by the moralists is ever revered".

Here the poet imagines that the beauty in question is automatically depicted on the rock in a miraculous manner as she is getting ready to die by leaping from the peak.

Respect and regard for moral values form part and parcel of a good life. It follows logically from this premise that these damsels in their capacity of good widows are worthy of honour, respect and regard.

Many a poet praises these beauties maintaining the view that they are about to commit suicide for the sake of their dear departed. The poets often notice many human values in them. They declare these beauties to be protecting their chastity as a great treasure.

A poet who visited the rock pays attention to all that, but he still has a question to pose, a question full of satire.

She has grieved
Over the dear departed
That she doth chatter
At this corner of that, no matter.
Yet she appears to leap
Into an abyss deep
If so, pray, why then
Does she prefer to be in the den?

The beauties are bereaved by the death of the king. Yet they are chattering in different corners. However, they also appear to be hurling themselves down from the rock. If so why do they continue to remain on the rock?

The poet implies that the damsels are pretending to leap from the peak. If they decide to terminate their lives through their great sorrow over the death of the king, what is it that prevents them from taking such a step? The beauties pretend to leap from the peak while engaged in chattering with one another in different corners. They pretend to be bereft by the death of the king merely to conform to the custom, but in fact they do not like to leave those who visit them and to die for the sake of their lover, the king.

The author of the verse No. 20 is not inclined to present a novel idea. He simply wonders as to how these damsels who are about to hurl themselves down could at all remain on the rock. Thus it is said:

20. නැගී බලුමො රන්වන් සිහිගිරි ගල්බිත්හි
හිඳි මෙහි කෙසෙ මෙන් ගලමතිනි හෙන්නයුන් [වැනි] හො

Nägī balumo ran-van Sihigiri gal-bit'hi
Hindi mehi kese men gala-matini hennayun [väni] ho

We ascended the rock and looked at the golden-coloured one on the rock wall of Sihigiri. How does (she) remain here, I wonder, – she who is like unto those falling down from the summit of the rock?

This is the sort of imagination that crops up in the fertile mind of a poet on noticing the different poses of the damsels on the rock.

309. බලයි මග මෙන් හො
(නැ)සී නො යි හිමි සමහර්හු වගුළො ගිරිබිතින්

Balayi maṅga piyā vana-vū-himin men ho
(Nä)sī no yi himi samaharhu vaguḷo giri-bitin

She, the dear one, gazes at the road in the manner of those whose lords have been separated from them. 'Did not (our) lord die?' So (thinking), the others hurled themselves down from the rock wall.

She is gazing at the road as if she is separated from her lover and there are others who realized that their lovers are dead and gone and so they too leap from the peak.

The author of the verse No.164 presents a poetic vision as follows:

164. අහො ජනිම් මම් පිරිජුන් සෙය් සිහිගිරි මොයුන්
නැවතෙන් අසද්නි නැවැතැ රසඇතියවුන් ඇත්තෙන්

Aho janim mam pirijun sey Sihigiri moyun
Nävaten asadni nävätä rasa-ätiyavun ätten

I know, alas, how Sihigiri has been ruined by these (people). Stop, O faithless ones, as there are, once more, people with (good) taste.

Here the poet says that Sihigiri has been made desolate due to a dearth of men of good taste. The ladies, thus feeling themselves neglected, are on the point of leaving the place. The writer exhorts them to remain behind as there are, once more, men of good taste. He himself, of course, was one of these connoisseurs.

A poet called Hela from Rukuli is laughing at the Sigiri damsels who are getting ready to hurl themselves from the peak:

510. මන් බුණ කලක් මත [දූකැ සි]හිගිරි ආ වෙ මා
ඔ වි නො පැනහි සෙ වලකයි ගිරි [න්]හෙනයු න් වැනි කා

Man buṇa kalak mata [däkä Si]higiri ā ve mā
O vi no päna-hi se valakayi giri[n] henayun väni kā

I came (back), having seen, on the summit of Sihigiri, a damsel whose pride has been shattered. She, who has the appearance of those falling down from the rock, is as if she is unable to leap (down), (for) who prevents (her from doing so)?.

The poet states three things. We may sum them up as follows:

I came back from Sigiri having seen a member of the fair sex with shattered pride. She has all the semblance of one who is leaping down from the rock, but she does not, in fact, fall down. Who or what is preventing her from doing so?

The origin of the Sinhala term "*man-bun*" is translated into English by Professor Paranavitana as "shattered pride" (whose pride has been shattered). But it may also be carefully interpreted to mean "one with a broken heart," as *man* may be either māna (pride) or mana – mind or heart.

It is quite possible that the poet arrived there in order to console the damsel with a broken heart. There is sufficient reason for the "heart-break", for the lover is far away from the damsel. The poet thought that the beauty was about to fall from the rock.

Although she appears to be getting ready to perform the rash act, does not in fact, leap from the peak. The poet thinks that it was one of the normal devices women adopted for the purpose of attracting the attention and sympathy of others. The poet says: "Hey you! there is nobody there to prevent you from leaping from the peak, so you had better do it."

The poet sees through the minds of women who say one thing but do something else. The poet considers the Sigiri damsels to be women with wavering minds, so he challenges them to perform the act which they appear to undertake.

One of the poets who reached Sigiri is lamenting over the harsh words leveled against the damsels by visiting poets. The following is his kind and friendly request to them:

Harshly he spoke of her, lo!
May you not do so.
Since these women meek
Having ascended the peak
Died there on account of their
Lover, the King,
Lanka's sovereign

Sigiri lingers in the memory
Of the poets who arrive there never weary.

It is true that one has spoken of them rashly and rudely. But may you not do so. Let us not forget that Sigiri has become famous because of these women, who having ascended the rock have also committed suicide on behalf of their lover by leaping from the peak.

These damsels are not free from fault and blemish. But isn't there a single benefit that can be credited to them? Sigiriya remains in our memory mainly because of these ladies who vowed to leap from the peak on behalf of their lover: the king of Sri Lanka. Hence, it does not behove you to censure them despite their petty faults.

The poet believes that the great memorial erected to commemorate *rasa* or the aesthetic taste is nothing but the psychological process of remembering over and over again that "thing of beauty is a joy for ever". This is proved beyond reasonable doubt by the fact that there are many and varied people who "cherish" and "relish" their sweet memories of Sigiriya even to-day. To remember over and over again – that is the immortal memorial of aesthetic enjoyment.

There are many and varied lyrics on the subject of "leaping from the peak." They remind us of one central theme of poetic significance. Our world is full of suffering and misery. In spite of this and, no doubt, with good training, a poet can enter *"rasa-loka',* the realm of aesthetic pleasure . This will enable him to experience a great aesthetic joy which is simultaneously both philosophical and transcendental in character. "A thing of beauty is a joy for ever".

The glory of Sigiriya resting on the presence of the *Apsaras,* the nymphs on the rock with name and fame wide-spread over a period of fifteen centuries clearly implies the splendour that was the picture wall and the grandeur that was the mirror wall.

SUGGESTIVE SILENCE

The Sigiri frescoes and the Sigiri poems have but one common source of artistic inspiration: the charm and beauty of the eternal female. In whatever manner the lovely living forms inspired the painters and generated the multitude of beauties that graced and glorified Sigiriya the Rock – so indeed did the same qualities of the Sigiriya damsels prompt the poetic concepts that were expressed in the lyrical compositions found there.

What has been depicted by the brush-strokes and by the stylus alike is nothing other than the animated quality which characterizes the damsels of Sigiriya.

Certain poets engaged in heart-to-heart talk. There was a favourable response. Though the others attempted to initiate conversation, they failed to elicit any response.

The Sigiri verses have been inspired by a minority of the Sigiri damsels. What they have in common is suggestive silence. They appear, however, to be pulsating with life. This inflamed the imagination of the poets and led them to expect a palpable response from the women.

60. බෙයදහි රන්වනුන් බියපත් මෙන් නො බැණැ සිටි
සිටි මල ගෙනැ අතින් මෙ දිගැස් තමන් නො බෙණෙත ජු

Beyadahi ran-vanun biya-pat men no bäṇä siṭi
Siṭi mala genä atin me digäs taman no beṇeta ju

'The golden coloured ones on the mountain side stand without speaking, as if (they are) frightened.' 'This long-eyed one, even though she does not herself speak, stands here, having taken a flower in (her) hand.'

The poet has not the slightest resentment against this damsel because of her silence. Though devoid of speech, she conveys her innermost feelings to the poet. How? By means of a flower in her hand. What does it not convey? These damsels are golden in colour. They are by the rock. The one who has approached them is a male. This particular damsel who is amongst the golden ones, though silent, stands there holding a flower.

While standing with the rest of them just imagine how she conveyed the willingness in her heart to the poet secretly! The exultation induced in the poet called Bud (of) A (mbaga) na-vatu, by the sight of a damsel holding a blue water-lily is expressed by the lines:

6. අ[ද]නෙ සිත ම කත මෙ මෙහි නො[මෙ] බිණි වි ද තෙපුල්
සිත අදනු බණ[නා] බඳු [මහනෙල්] ගෙනැ ඇති හෙයින්
අ(මබග)ණවතු බුද්මි ලීමි

A[da]ne sita ma kata me mehi no[me] biṇi vi da tepul
Sita adanu baṇa[nā] bandu [mahanel] genä äti heyin
A(mbaga)ṇa-vatu Budmi līmi

Though (she) did not speak a word, this damsel here attracts my mind; as she has taken water-lilies (in her hand), she attracts one's mind as if she were speaking.

Though the lady does not engage in conversation, she has gripped my heart. Her very pose holding the flower suggests that she is engaged in a heart-to-heart talk with me; that is how my mind is entrapped. For the mind's allurement towards a lady, one should give ear to her sweet words.

However much she may be of exquisite beauty, it is through her words, that one could recognize what sort of heart she possesses. The attraction towards her is due to the fact that she is holding a blue water-lily quite expressive of her feelings. The poet is not the least hampered by her silence, for, she is holding in her hand a cluster of flowers that is expressive enough!

The Private Secretary of Prince Mihidal, the poet Bohodevi blames or implores a fair damsel who has committed an unworthy act:

119. සපුකුසුම් සුරත්නි ගත් හෙළිලබියුක
මන ම තමහට් නමය් ම හය් නො මෙ බුණු අනියා

Supu-kusum surat-atni gat heḷilabiyuka
Mana ma tamahaṭ namay ma hay no me buṇu aniyā

A fair damsel, who has taken a Sapu flower in her exceedingly rosy hand, having bent my mind towards her, did not speak to me. (That is) unjust.

A damsel with a fair complexion holding a cluster of champak - flowers in her rosy hand has seized my mind and kept it with her. But she did not talk with me. That is not right on her part. Having shown champak-flowers signifying gestures of love, the damsel attracted the mind of the poet towards her. Having done so, her bounden duty would have been to engage in a pleasant dialogue.

Without leaving him alone to mind his own business is it right on her part, to excite him and then refrain from talking to him?

The poet by the name of *Nadamal* while composing a poem, comments on the silence of a Sigiriya damsel. The skill shown by the poet in presenting the situation and the theme is quite appealing.

235. අමතයි තොප අයුත් මහනෙල්වනින් එක් [ජ]න්
ඇති වී ද නොබණන වන් දැකැ ආ අත මල් තිපි
නදමල් ම ගියු ගී

Amatayi topa ayut mahanel-vanin ek [ja]n
Äti vī da no-baṇana van däkä ā ata mal tipi
Nada-mal ma giyu gī

O lily-coloured ones, know that one has come (here) and addressed you. Though there was the appearance that (you) do not speak, (he) came having seen the flowers in your hands.

You should know that the one who came here casting a glance at you, is anxious to get a word from you. O! damsels, glowing with blue water-lily complexion, please know that I am talking to you. Though there seems to be a tendency on your part not to speak, we were compelled by the flowers in your hands to visit you.

Though the number of words the poet uses is very small, there is not the slightest flaw in the word-picture.

The poet is drawing closer to the damsel. But she is standing there in some sort of seeing-and-unseeing attitude. It seems that the conversation has been started by the poet. At the outset, he has directed her attention towards him by talking to her, and then he reproves her slightly. Now he has a right to speak to her sternly. For, his visit here is an outcome of the gesture given by the hand holding clusters of flowers. If the poet's words are translated into modern colloquial usage it would go something like this:

'Here is a girl like a blue water-lily. There someone is talking. Though there is a tendency, on her part, to avoid conversation, one could understand her message. I have not just come here, without an invitation. For, I was fully aware of the language of the flower in her hand!'

The poets understood the silent attitudes of the damsels despite the absence of dialogue. The literary devices which they made use of to convey their sentiments to the readers vary considerably. Though the ideas expressed are based on the same theme, the content and form vary according to the poetic vision, knowledge of life, and the inventive power of each poet.

Because certain poets, well-versed in poetic tenets and full of worldly wisdom, have presented the contents in a remarkable manner, pertaining to canons of appropriate poetic forms, the readers have inherited a collection of lyrical poems full of suggestion and sentiment evoking *'Rasa'* or taste. This is a collocation of verses reflected in the Mirror-wall,that is made up of wisdom and sentiment of ever-lasting value which sharpens the sensibility of the reader.

Let me examine here, the delicate synthesis of words made use of by the Ruhunu poet called (Dala) Siv, to convey his feelings with regard to Sigiriya damsels who were rather reluctant to respond:

26. ඇවිජ් (මුයුන්) බලත් බෙයඳ් (කිස්හි) රන්වනුන්
බැලුම් මුත් අන් තෙපුල් නොදුන් නුයුනින් නිසසල

Ävij (muyun) balat beyand-(kis'hi) ran-vanun
Bälum mut an tepul no-dun nuyunin nisasala

When we came and looked at these golden-coloured ones in the cavity on the mountain side, (they) gave no other speech but glances from their motionless eyes.

When we came here, and were looking at the golden damsels on the rock, they only looked at us with motionless eyes, without uttering any words. Here our attention should be directed to the poet's use of word *'an tepul'*. Now compare and contrast the two-fold expressions.

'Nisasala nuyunin balum mut an tepul no-dun'
'Nisasala nuyunin balum mut tepul no-dun'

The second one implies that they looked at them with motionless eyes but never engaged in conversation. However, the poet was able to understand the messages in their eyes, suggesting 'speech' or 'utterancc' given by the act of looking. What the poet has expressed is that he has had no dialogue other than an exchange of glances. It looks as if the poet has been afforded an opportunity for the communication of a quite personal or confidential message through her glance. The magic here is created by the appropriate use of '*an*' in *an tepul* which elevates *balum* too to an act of speech!

In abstruse poetical conceptions of this type there is a wider meaning or a double image, over and above the direct expression. Until one comprehends it clearly, it is rather difficult to enjoy the *'Rasa'* or taste or the suggestion and sentiment involved in it.

If one fails to get at the hidden meaning – which is the most noteworthy characteristic in the poetry of Sigiriya, one might not grasp the suggested significance or the intended meaning, particularly if one fails to perceive the indications presented in the poems:

(i) multiple image (ii) indirect reference (iii) sophisticated expressions etc., the poetry may appear as, 'void-verse' as already pointed out by a certain Sigiriya poet. There is a poem which states: 'even if I speak she does not speak'.

21. සපු [මල] නිළිබදල ගත හෙළිලලබුයකු මන
මයි දි නෙත තමා මෙ බල (ඇ)ත ම බණවත නො බෙණෙයි

Sapu-[mala] niḷiba-dala gata heḷillabuyaku mana
Mayi di neta tamā me bala (ä)ta ma baṇa-vata no beṇeyi

A fair damsel who has taken sapu flowers and lotus buds (in her hand) has herself looked (at me), giving me her mind (as well as her) eye; but (she) speaks not even when I call her.

'A fair damsel holding in her hand champak flowers and lotus buds having offered her mind and eyes to me is looking at me. Even if I speak she is speechless.' This fair damsel has offered her mind and the eye to the poet.

She is looking in the direction of the poet. She is holding the champak-flowers and lotus buds with their insinuations or implications of love! So, what am I to say? The meaning involved here may be this. 'Though I speak to her driven by sheer folly (*'ma bana – vata'*), there seems to be nothing left to speak on.'

One poet has stated that because of his failure to perform meritorious deeds in his previous birth and acquire merit, these damsels were rather reluctant to speak to him.

40. තොප නුයුන් මහනෙල් විය ද ම හෙ නැ පැහැදියෙ
ම නොකෙළෙයින් තම න් පින් දැන් මට තොප නුදුන් බස

Topa nuyun mahanel viya da ma he nä pähädiye
Ma no-keḷeyin tama n pin dän maṭa topa nudun basa

Your eyes are water-lilies; but that (fact) did not satisfy me. Good deeds have not been performed by myself (in previous births); speech has, therefore, not been given to me by you.

Poet Sangapala has stated that one damsel with motionless eyes whose tendency is not to speak when spoken to, looked at him.

17. (ප)ලාව(තු)වෙ[ලැ] අරමබ් තැනූ සඟපල්(බතී)මි මෙ ගී ලීමි
බෙයඥ් ගොසින් බැලූමො සිත් සුරුැස්නා සෙය්
බණතුජ් නොබෙණෙනන් ඇ[සිපි] යෙව් එයුන් ලයු නැත්තේ

(Pa)lāva(tu)-ve[lä] aramb tänū Saṅgapal-(batī)mi me gī līmi
Beyand gosin bälūmo sit surusnā sey
Banat=uj no-beṇenan ä[si-pi] yev eyun layu nätte

We went to the mountain side and, in such manner as the mind becomes well pleased, looked at these(i.e. the women) who do not speak even when (we) speak (to them). Of them, indeed, there is not (even) the falling of eyelids.

Another poet says:

181. සනාගනවූයුන් වනවූසෙයින් මෙ තමන්
බණවත් ද නො මෙ බෙණෙත් ගෙණෙත් සිකි මොයුන් අසදුන් අතුරෙ

Sanā-gana-vūyun vana-vū-seyin me taman
Baṇavat da no me beṇet geṇet siki moyun asadun ature

(The women) whose affection has been frozen, just as they have become widows, do not speak at all even when (others) speak (to them). They will, O friend, be counted among the faithless ones.

Poet Midhalu Dal says in verse 140:

140. අසය තොප අයුතින් මෙ දක්නා රිසින් ආ
සැබැවින් සසැඳලි කළයුන් බැවින් ම හය් නො බුණු

Asaya topa ayutin me daknā risin ā
Säbävin sasändali kaḷayun bävin ma hay no buṇu

As (you) are (women) who have contracted a union in an honourable manner, (you) did not speak to me who came here with the desire of seeing (you), even though I came here because I had heard of you.

149. ඇවිදූ දුරකතර් එ [ගි]ය මෙන් පැතු සිතු ජැහි
දුට් ජ මා ඇස් පුරා ලද මෙන් බස [නො] වී තී

Ävidä dura-katar e [gi]ya men pätu situ jähi
Duṭ ja mā äs purā lada men basa [no] vī tī

Having come to that remote wilderness, it is as if that which has been wished (for) and thought (about) has become forsaken. Though (you have) been seen to the entire satisfaction of my eyes, it was not (so satisfying) as if a word of yours had been received (by me).

157. මෙලෙසි වී මා [ද]සු සි[වි]න් කෙළිබසක් [නැ]ත [ද]
(මෙහි) [සිත් සෙය්] අ(ව ම) බෙ[ය]ඳ්හි රන්(වනුන් අතරෙ)

Me-lesi vī mā [da]su si[vi]n keḷi-basak [nä]ta [da]
(Mehi) [sit sey] a(va ma) be[ya]nd'hi ran-(vanun atare)

When I come, according to my wish, into the midst of the golden-coloured ones on the mountain side here, I have, in this manner, become a slave (to them) because of their smile, though there is no playful speech (of theirs).

Though they are devoid of fun and frolic, the poet is captivated by their smiles. These ladies who are without speech are not moulded by any feeling; they smile just for the sake of smiling!

The Poet Pota Devu in his poem says:

136. පොත [ෙ]දවු ගී
සිව යි සිවිපත තෙපුල රහස බෙලුම් නැත්තන්
ගෙහෙනි ගයෙ ත කෙ නම් බෙයදහි අදහ ගත සිටුවයි

Pota D[e]vu gī
Siva yi sivi-pata tepula rahasa belum nättan
Geheni gaye ta ke nam beyadahi adaha gata siṭuvayi

(The women) who have no speech and no secret looks smiled because (others) smiled at them. What (wonder) is it that you went away, leaving behind (your) wife on the mountain side, and were quite at ease in your mind?

65. වැහැවෙත් කිසෙය් බෙයදහි රන්වනුන් දුටුවො
සිවියු(ද) [ෙ]තපුල නැත (උන්) රහසට [නො] බෙයද අතුරෙ [සිටි]

Vähävet kisey beyadahi ran-vanun duṭuvo
Siviyu(da) t[e]pula näta (un) rahasaṭa [no] beyada ature [siṭi]

In what manner can those who have seen the golden-coloured ones on the mountain side bear themselves up? Though (they) smiled, there is no speech from them. Is it not for the sake of secrecy that they remained in the midst of the mountain side?

In this manner they vividly express how fascinated they are by the silence of the damsels.

Kital invites a mute Sigiriya damsel:

52. තා නු[යු]න [මහනෙ]ල [බෙය]ඳැහි සිටි [හෙළිල්ලම්බි]
දසන් මිණිතරින් අලු ජ හජ බැණැ ලන් තම [ෙ]ස[මෙ]න්

Tā nu[yu]na [mahane]la [beya]ndahi siṭi [heḷillambi]
Dasan miṇi-tarin alu ja haja bäṇä lan tama s[eme]n

Oh! Fair damsel standing on the mountain side, even though the blue water-lily of your eye has been illuminated with the lustre of the jewels which are your teeth, do speak (out) your heart gently.

This fair damsel is looking at the blue water-lily which she is holding. While looking at it, she smiles. Through the lustre of her smile, even the flower is glowing. The damsel does not raise her head, even to have a look at the poet.

In this verse '*nu[yu]na[mahane] la*' has been interpreted as blue-water lily eye. In this case the poet might not have imagined that her eyes glimmered by the lustre of her smile. The two words '*nuyuna van mahanela*' are far more precise than the two words '*nuyuna mahanela*' for she is smiling at the blue lotus.

A monk by the name of Daham-senal, a resident of Mana pirivena, is under the impression that these damsels show entirely different attitudes towards different persons.

189. මානාපිරිවනවැසි දහම්සෙනල් [පැවි]ජ්[ජන් ගී]
හිඳි [ෙ]ස ගලැ ක[තුන්]ත එත තුළුළෙන් (සෙයි) වී
[බ]ලයි මයි එ රන්වන් නො [මෙ] බිණි සෙයි වියොවු සෙයි

Mānā-pirivana-väsi Daham-senal [pävi]j[jan gī]
Hindi s[e] galä-ka[tun] ta eta tuḷuḷen (seyi) vī
[Ba]layi mayi e ran-van no [me] biṇi seyi viyovu seyi

When you come, the manner in which the lovely women remained on the rock is as if (they were) in love. The manner in which the self-same golden-coloured ones, having looked at me, did not speak, is like unto that of those separated (from their lovers).

Although their responses are varied the poet conveys that when the damsels saw him approaching, though he was enamoured, while looking at him, they behaved as if they were afflicted by separation. (that is because of the fact that he is a monk).

Though unaware of the condition, the poets, inquired as to why they do not converse. Maganava Sen, who was aware of the condition explains the reason:.

198. තමන් පිය නට් සෙවින් අදන් වැ නොබණනන්
මොයුන් බෙයන්ඳ්හි අද්හ යෙත් (බණ)ත අ(ප හය්) නොදහම්
මගණවැ සෙ(න්මි)

Taman piya naṭ sevin adan vä nobaṇanan
Moyun beyand'hi- ad'ha yet (baṇa)ta a (pa hay) no-daham
Magaṇavä Se(nmi)

These people go to the mountain side, having faith in those who, being afflicted with grief on account of the ruin of their lover, do not speak. If they do speak with us, it would not be a virtuous act.

In poem 137 the poet has stated that they ascend the rock and while they were looking at Sigiriya, the damsels have given signs without directly saying that they are speechless or, that one should refrain from talking to them. The poem is written to indicate how one should behave before them. It is indeed a remarkable creation, presented from an entirely different viewpoint.

137. නැගී සන් දෙව හෙ නො වෙ සිග්සෙ පනත්
බ[ණ] සඟරෙන් නිගොම් තුබු අත්පාසලකුණින්

Näg(ī) san deva he no ve sig-se panat
Ba[ṇa] saṅgaren nigom tubu at-pā-salakuṇin

Ascend (the rock) and give a signal. That (too) is not proper (if it is done) speedily. Speak noiselessly with signs of the hands and feet, settled by mutual agreement.

Here the poet does not suggest that the lady is mute. If it is necessary to speak that should be done silently in a courteous manner, by symbolic gestures of hands and feet.

One of the poets say that the golden-coloured one is rather speechless and that his intention is not to go back.

163. නො යන්නෙ ආ යහපත් ද රන්වන් බලත මෙ
නො යන්නෙ මා (පැහැපත්) රන්වන් ම හය් නෙ බෙණෙත

No yanne ā yahapat da ran-van balata me
No yanne mā (pähäpat) ran-van ma hay no beṇeta

'Is he happy when he looks at this golden-coloured one that (the person) who has come here does not go (away)? 'I do not go away as the resplendent golden-coloured one speaks not with me.'

The monk Riyansen keeping with his monastic position gives some advice to the Sigiriya damsels. However, in this advice there appears to be an underlying sarcasm:

128. උක[ැ]ටැලි (වි) අ[යි]මි උකැටැලි බලනට නවත
තුප උකැටැලි දිනි බෙයදැහි රනවනනි නො බණ

Uk[ä]ṭäli (vi) a[yi]mi ukäṭäli balanaṭa navata
T[u]pa ukäṭäli dini beyadahi rana-vanani no baṇa

I came here having become despondent. To those who see this, (there will be) despondency. You gave rise to despondency again. O golden-coloured ones on the mountain side, (pray) do not speak.

This monk is in an apathetic mood. The apathy is further increased, by beholding the damsels for taking no notice of the visiting monk. By any chance if they spoke they might have furnished reasons either to increase the apathetic attitude of the monk or prompt him to leave his monastery and turn to worldly pleasures. Hence, it was better for them to have been mute.

The poet, who composed the verse 203 in response to the above, states that he looked at the damsels, without any type of aloofness, and that as they were devoid of speech he did not speak to them.

203. බැලූමො රිසි සෙය් උකැ ටැ ලී ජැහැ යෙහෙන්
බෙයන්ද්හි රන්වනු බිණිය නො හෙයෙන් ම නො බිණියෙ

Bä lūmo risi sey ukä ṭa lī jähä yehen
Beyand'hi ran-vanu biṇiya no heyen ma no biṇiye

Having discarded despondency, (we) according to our desire, looked at the golden-coloured one on the mountain side with happiness. As (she) is unable to speak, I did not speak.

The verse written by the King named Mapurama, seems to be some sort of eulogy, when taken superficially, but it contains a deep sarcasm:

143. එ මළ ද නො බණය සහනෙ මෙ කිම නම
කළ යි පි න ත පවසමො හිමබ අකමය වය

E maḷa da no baṇaya sahane me kima nama
Kaḷa yi pi na ta pavasamo himaba akamaya vaya

'Though (he) is dead, there is endurance (in you), without speaking. What (conduct) is this? We declare that meritorious deeds have been performed by you (in your previous existence). O, (my) lady, forgive me.'

Though their husband has passed away, these ladies maintain perfect silence without crying or weeping. Can the strong-willed ladies bear it in that way? If they could do so it may be an outcome of the meritorious deeds which they have performed in their previous births.

When considering the differing views expressed by poets concerning the Sigiriya damsels – their alleged treacherousness, their rude refusal to reply when spoken to and so on – the idea expressed by the poet Buyuru Kasaba appears to be an '*Anyalapa*' (Skt) *an alap,* (Sinhala) an allegorical metaphor.

187. රතඅත පලු[ම]ලෙන අබුළ ළපතක සෙයි ලි මෙ
[බිණි]වි සැබ[වින] හිමබුසු නොබණනනො කී නොවදන

Rata-ata palu-[ma]lena abuḷa ḷa-pataka seyi li me
[Biṇi]vi säba[vina] himabuyu no-baṇanano kī no-vadana

'This damsel, like unto a fluttering tender bud, in fact spoke with the buds and flowers in her hand; it is (therefore) an untrue word that has been said: 'The ladies do not speak'.

The poet here stresses the fact that the damsels really speak. Though they do not let their words escape their lips to express ideas or emotions, they do give vent to them. They convey them through the medium of flowers and buds which they hold in their hands. Though they show some sort of restraint by being silent, they fulfill their mind's desire by other means.

In the interpretation given to this particular verse, one is at a loss to understand the phrase 'they spoke with buds and flowers' They do not speak with buds and flowers, they speak with people, not with their mouths, *'Rata –ata palumalena',* but through the medium of buds and flowers in their rosy hands.

The poet named Badagiri Pasili is asking a question from the speechless damsels. He gets replies as well.

208. බල හිමබුනි අසද් ඇසිමු ජො[ෙ]හා නො බණනා
බණවත නො මෙ බණන්නුමු හි(ද) ගල කෙළෙයින් සි ගිරි

Bala himabuni asad äsimu joh(o) no baṇanā
Baṇavata no me baṇannumu hi(da) gala keḷeyin Si giri

'Look (here, you) faithless ladies, we asked whether you do not, indeed, speak.' 'We, indeed, do not speak, even though (people) speak (to us), as Sigiri has turned our hearts (into) stone.'

As the damsels refrain from speaking the poet aroused by wrath, questioned them as to why the treacherous ladies are so mute. The ladies then break their silence. As the Sigiriya rock made our heart stony, we do not speak even if you speak to us.

But, Poet Mati of Elene has a different attitude towards the golden coloured ones:

1. බෙයඳ් අවැජ් නොලද් එක ගීයක් [කියී මා]
[බස]ක් රන්වනැන් වනැන් බැලිමි අසිරි සිහිගිරී

Beyand aväj no-lad ek gīyak [kiyī mā]
[Basa]k ran-vanän vanän bälimi asiri Sihigirī

Not a word from the golden-coloured ones, who are seperated (from their lover) has been obtained by me for having recited one song after having come to the mountain side. I, (therefore), looked at the wonders of Sihigiri.

FAME AND GLORY OF THE LION KING

The thoughts of most of the poets who scribbled verses on the Sigiriya Mirror-wall were attracted by the painted emotive female figures. These subtle figures moved the hearts of the poets in those days more than did the other creations such as palaces, tanks and ponds that adorned Sigiriya and its neighbourhood. On the other hand, these figures transmitted a warm, intimate quality associated with life's experiences which is not implicit in the other man-made and natural features of Sigiriya. Most poets, therefore were happy and contented to be in the company of the frescoes and composed poems about them.

However, the lion figure, the ponds, the parks and the like, deemed incomparable creations, were also themes for certain poets. There were poets who did not take any special notice of the female figures but were enamoured by the mammoth lion figure.

Except for the two fore-paws of the lion, the rest of the body is now destroyed. Archaeologists up to date have not discovered anything which can be considered its remains. It is therefore rationalized by some that King Kassapa did not create a lion figure in Sigiriya but only the front paws were carved in conformity with the lion figure on the rock.

It is not rational to arrive at such subjective conclusions without studying reliable sources such as the Sigiriya verses. The Sigiriya poets lived at a time very close to the date of Sigiriya's creation. There is a substantial number of Sigiriya poems on the Lion figure which bear eloquent testimony to prove the futility of such arguments limiting the figure of the lion to it's fore-paws alone.

The lion's figure linked to the name of the Sinhala nation was undoubtedly a creation of immense inspiration. The name Sigiriya itself proves the pride of place given to the figure of the lion there.

The following is a poem among others expressing the emotionally excited thoughts of a poet after seeing the lion figure:

45. නැගී ඇති බලනට බැලිමි සිහිමියන් සිහිගිරි
මනදෙළ පුරය් ඇති බලනරිසි [නො]වෙ බෙයන්ද් රන්වන්

Nägī äti balanaṭa bälimi si-himiyan Sihigiri
Manadoḷa puray äti balana-risi [no]ve beyand-ran-van

Having ascended Sihigiri to see what is(there), I fulfilled my mind's desire and saw His Lordship the Lion. There is no desire (in me) to look at the golden-coloured one on the cliff.

Does it imply that seeing the lion is limited to seeing the paws of the lion? Another poet creates a charming figure of speech on the enormous height of the lion and its fearlessness.

174. (අ)[වු]ද් මුළු වෙ ගිරිහි යන වී අප මුළු විසිරි
[සි]හිදුන් සෙය හැඟැ අප සිහි වන්නට් සිහිගිරි

(A)[vu]d muḷu ve girihi yana vī apa muḷu visiri
[Si]hid=un seya hä(ṅ)gä apa sihi vannaṭ Sihigirī

Having come here, (the people) become crowded (together) on the rock. The lord of lions it seems, felt (this) and stood (here) in order that we may scatter ourselves from the crowd and go away, and also to secure that Sihigiri shall be impressed on our memory.

The people arrived and assembled on the summit of the rock. The lion king understood this and stood as if to disperse (the crowd) and imprint on our memories the grandeur of Sigiriya.

One poet mentions that he saw both the lion king and the blue-lily eyed maidens:

205. සීරජු යසස සිරී තුබූ මුළුලොව් පැතිරී
නිලුපුල්ඇසුන් අසිරී බැලූමො සිහිගිරී

Sī-raju yasasa sirī tubū muḷu-lov pätirī
Nilupul-äsun asirī bälūmo Sihigirī

We saw at Sihigiri the king of lions, whose fame and splendour remain spread in the whole world, and the wonderful damsels with eyes (like) blue lilies.

Verse number 346 is a composition which deftly shows the appreciation of the Sigiriya ladies and the Lion King at the same time.

346. මෙහි [ජ] නා මෙ කරන පියවි ද [සි]රජුන් ඇරැ
නුවනින්ඳ්නිල්මිණි තොප දකුත් නො මෙ ඇසිරැ කළමො

Mehi [ja]nā me karana piyavi da [si]-rajun ärä
Nuvan=ind-nil-miṇi topa dakut no me äsirä kaḷamo

This, which the people are doing here, leaving aside His Majesty the Lion - is it natural?' 'When we saw the blue sapphires of your eyes, we did not, indeed, pay court (to him)'.

The ladies in the paintings seeing numerous people coming towards them ask 'Aren't they engaged in a futile exercise in coming here leaving the lion king'? The people answer 'when we see your blue-sapphire hued eyes we do not desire the company of the lion.'

The Sigiriya poets who saw through the feminine mind were maddened by the enticing nature of the damsels and created poetry focusing on their beauty. However, some poets estimated the splendour of the lion greater than the splendour of the damsels. Some describe how the lustre of the gem-like eyes of the damsels obliterate the majesty of the Lion King.

One poet after seeing the Sigiri long-eyed ones (ladies) and the lion emphasises that the item that must be seen is the lion.

476. [දි]ගැ[ස්] ගිරිහිසැ හිඳි ඇවිද් මෙ ග[ල] බැලුමො
[බ]ලමනා තක් ඇවි[ද්]බැලුමො සී සිහිගිරි

[Di]gä[s] giri-hisä hindi ävid me ga[la] bälumo
[Ba]lamanā tak ävi[d] balumo sī Sihigirī

'Having come to this rock, we looked at the long-eyed one who remained on the summit of the rock.' 'We came and looked at the Lion of Sihigiri – all that is worth looking at.'

Vajur Agboy, the poet living in the residence of the lady known as Sata climbed the rock, took part in festivities and says in verse 286 how all these happened due to the efficacy of the lion's powers:

286. ගල්මුඳුන් නැගි බැලිමි බෙයඳැ මා සිත්
රෙපෙ දුන් මගුල් කෙළෙමි සිහිමියා බැලැනි වි

Gal-mundun nägī bälīmi beyandä mā sit
Repe dun magul keḷemi sī-himiyā bäläni vī

I ascended the summit of the rock and looked at (things). On the mountain side I celebrated festivities which (as it were) gave form to my thoughts. All this came to pass through the might of His Majesty the Lion.

576. අතින් [ම]ල් ගත් කලු මෙ දුට පවහි සිරෙ වෙ[යි]
සිහිමියන් ත[ම]න් දුට නො [වන්]නෙ යි [සිහි] තම [හට]

Atin [ma]l gat kalu me duṭa pavahi sire ve[yi]
Si-himiyan ta[ma]n duṭa no [van]ne yi [sihi] tama[haṭa]

When this damsel, who has taken flowers in her hand, is seen, one gets imprisoned on the rock. When his Lordship the Lion is seen by one, (the lion) does not become remembered.

This poet means that anyone seeing the lady with the flowers in her hands will become imprisoned in the rock. A person seeing the Lion will be so frightened that he will not remember him.

It is necessary to examine further whether the poet wanted to convey this idea. There seems to be no logical connection between the two expressions 'seeing the lady, one is imprisoned in the rock' and 'seeing the lion, he will not remember him or will be out of his senses.' What did the poet want to say? Was it that the poet's thoughts are imprisoned in the rock after seeing the lady and that when seeing the lion, his thoughts about the lady disappear?

It is clear from the form of the poem that the poet wanted to show the greater attractiveness of the lion in comparison with the lady. It is a good poetic turn of phrase and imagery to say that the lady who is capable of imprisoning a person by her beauty is forgotten by seeing the lion.

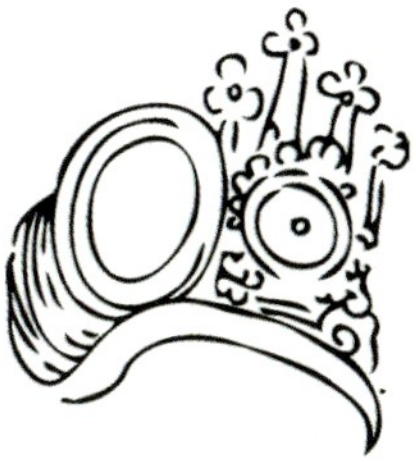

THUS SHONE THE LAKE IN SPLENDOUR

It was the lovely Sigiri damsels who captured the hearts of the majority of visitors to Sigiriya. Although the lion figure was an impressive artistic creation, it was to the intrinsic beauty of the lake rather than to the majesty and splendour of the former that the attention of some of the poets was drawn. The extent to which they were excited and captured by those feminine forms finds expression in their poetic creations.

In verse No. 4 of Paranavitana's Sigiri Graffiti, poet Agbo Himi gives the description of the Sigiri lake; even after the lapse of several centuries, it is capable of conveying the quality of the poet's heart and ecstatic enjoyment blended with aesthetic pleasure in an experience of sheer delight.

4. [නැ]ගි අලුයම අවුජ් බලය් සිටියිනි මෙහි මය්
විදිමි මනැමරු ගස එත තමු(රු)වෙනෙහි සුවනු (මෙහි)

[Nä]gi aluyama avuj balay siṭiyini mehi may
Vindimi manda-maru gasa eta tamu(ru)-venehi suvand (mehi)
[himiyemi me] gī līmi

As I, having climbed (up), came here at dawn and stood looking at (this), I enjoy the fragrance of the clusters of lotuses as the gentle breeze comes blowing here.

The words employed here in the ninth century, to express this genuine heart-felt aesthetic experience differ but little from the turn of phrase of today. If this verse were to be translated in to the language of today it would need only slight alteration.

නැගි අලුයම අවුත්
බලා සිටියෙන් මෙහි මම
විඳිමි මඳ මරු ගස එන
තඹුරු වෙනෙහි සුවඳ මෙහි

The only difference here is that ස (sa) in ගස (gasa) cannot be lengthened.

A certain poet climbs the hill in order to see the Sigiri damsels. But he finds it impossible to make the journey. On the way, another damsel catches his eye. This poetical idea is expressed in verse 580.

580. මලඅකරෙ එත පැහැසර් තොයිනි තිසරන් මො වෙ
විලම්බු මන ම තමහට මෙ ගත වන තකා අය කොට

Mala-akare eta pähäsar toyini tisaran mo ve
Vilambu mana ma tamahaṭa me gata vana takā aya koṭa

When the swans come from the clear water to the flowers and (tender) buds, this Lake Lady has taken my mind to herself alone, as if (I am) one come (here) intent on the forest.

The swans move gently across the water to the flowers and buds. The poet too makes his way across the wood towards the Sigiri damsel. Dame Lake did not think the poet was intent upon seeing the fair damsels, but the wood, and so won his heart. If she did know that he was intent upon seeing another damsel, Dame Lake would have kept silent.

The lake's beauty was so irresistible that the poet was unable to visit the damsels of Sigiri without first having visited the lake.

That Dame Nal, wife of Lord Mahamet, was not so impressed as to give such a description of Sigiri lake; this is illustrated by this song that she composed:

543. මහමෙත්හිමියා අබු නාල් හිමියබුයුන් ග ලියු [මෙ] ගී
නො ජනම්හ මුන් මිහි විලබු කුම් ජැයක් ආව
මෙ ලියපියෙ එයුන් මෙ තමන් දිවි යවි යි පවසා

Mahamet-himiyā abu Nāl himiyabuyun ga liyu [me] gī
No janamha mun mihi vilabu kum jäyak āva
Me liya-piye eyun me taman divi yavi yi pavasā

Whatever thing came (into being) of the Lake Lady, we do not know (why) this (stanza) was written down here by these persons, after having themselves proclaimed that their life would pass away.

Dame Nal does not admire the maidens of Sigiri and therefore, she questions why these men make such an issue of a lake when there are lovely damsels to talk about.

In verse 582 the poet says:

මත්බමරුගුළ ඇවිලි [නො]මඳ් ලොළ වී කිහුමු
ගුමම්නි මල්කෙසුර නොසුකසු කළ යි හැමූ
කුමුඳ්වන විද්හෙ [වී සරා] සිසිරැස් හමූ
නුයුළ වී ඇ[ය] නැති යි එය් නො වී අපි යමු

Mat-bamar=uguḷa ävili [no]-mand loḷa vī kihumu
Gumamnī mal-kesura no-suk=asu kaḷa yi hämū
Kumund-vana vid'he [vī sarā]-sisi-räs hamū
Nuyuḷa vī ä[ya] näti yi ey no vī api yamū

The intoxicated bee, having been excessively greedy of the flower, became entrapped and, (thinking) that the filament of the flower brought it to grief, bit (it), humming (the while). Clusters of white water-lilies, having encountered the beams of the autumnal moon, become expanded. (But) she has not become well disposed; so, we go away, not having become like that.

When the autumn moon has risen in the sky at night, a poet approaches the damsels of Sigiri. Clusters of white water lillies were then in bloom. It is the exquisite beauty of Sigiri lake that attracted the imagination of a poet to give expression to such a thought.

In the meantime, the poet observes another incident. Having being excessively lured by the flower, the bee, not realising that time is running out, is entrapped within it. The poet too, though well aware of the circumstances, is about to suffer the same fate. If, on such a late evening, the poet were to tarry longer on account of these maidens, there is every possibility that the fate that befell the bee would overtake him as well. So realising it, one should be cautious in such an enticing situation and depart from the scene, leaving the maidens to themselves.

The wondrous beauty of Sigiri Lake is suggestively conveyed in a verse composed in the form of a dialogue between the poet and another writer who has gone into such raptures over the beauty of Sigiriya that he could go no further than the lake.

589 යෙහෙනි තමා පුයුත් කෙසෙ මෙ කි [වි] ඇ [ස දු]ට් මෙන්
නොහී බෙයන්ද් නැගී දැකැ [දි]සි මෙ[හි] විල සිරින් මෙ කී

Yeheni tamā puyu-t kese me ki [vi] ä[sa du]ṭ men
No-hī beyand nägī däkä [di]si me[hi] vila sirin me kī

'Though you have drunk of happiness, how has this been said as if (you have) seen with (your own) eyes, (though) not having been able to climb the mountain side and see?' 'This has been said (by me) for the splendour of the lake which is to be seen here.'

The prime object of this verse, expressed in the form of a dialogue, is to describe the visual beauty of Sigiri Lake. The poet's objective has been achieved by the delicate use of an unparalleled poetic device. The only mention of the lake is just one brief sentence "For the lake's evident splendour have I said so." The structure of the verse, however, conveys to the sensitive reader that much has been stated regarding Sigiriya's matchless beauty. It is possible that such sentiments prompted the dialogue between the two.

"I was greatly thrilled by the sight of Sigiri"
"Even without ascending the hill and not having
observed its beauty with (your own) eyes, how do
you say you were thrilled?"

Thus did the poet convey the sentiment that one could be thrilled merely by the sight of the lake, without having encountered any other feature of Sigiriya.

The quatrain 558 on Sigiri lake takes the form of a description given by the brothers, Narayana and Mara:

558. යහජ සහළා [වූ] අනන්මන මියුර් යහ බසු
මහනෙල්හි නිල්කැලුම් තොපි රහසනි නෙත් දි ගැසු
සරාසිරිපුල්විලැ බ[ල]නෙ සිකිරින් මත් කළ [හ]සු
යෙහෙළි යහ කල කි බසින් [ඔ] දවරැය් එයින් නො බුසු

Yahaja sahaḷā [vū] ananmana miyur yaha basu
Mahanelhi nil-kälum topi rahasani net di gäsu
Sarā-siri-pul-vilä ba[la]ne sikirin mat kaḷa-[ha]su
Yeheḷi yaha kala ki basin [o] dava-räy eyin no busu

Paranavitana renders this stanza as follows:

Sweet and auspicious speeches to one another,
worthy of their goodness of heart, were(there), (to wit:) 'Having cast your glance (at them) in secret, the blue lustre of the water-lilies has been vanquished by you'. 'Do look at the black swan, overjoyed by the spray, in the lake which has flowered with the splendour of autumn'. Due to the auspicious and clever speech uttere by (her) confidante, she did not, day or night, get down from there.

Nandasena Mudiyanse's Sinhala rendering of the verse is as follows:

'හොඳ සිරිත් ද මිත්‍ර ලීලාවෙන් ද (යුතු) අන්‍යෝන්‍යයන් කෙරෙහි (පැවැති) මධුර යහපත් වචන (ඇත්තේ) විය. රහසින් (ඔවුන් හට) නෙත දී තෙපි මහනෙල්හි නිල් කැලුම් ගැසුවාහු ය. ශරත් ශ්‍රීයෙන් පිපුණු විලෙහි මුවරදින් මත් වු කළ හසුන් බලන්න.
යෙහෙළි කී යහපත් කාන්ත වචන නිසා ඕ තොමෝ දිවා රාත්‍රි එයිත් නො බැස්සාය.'

(සීගිරි ගී ද්විතීය භාගය 265 පිටුව)

The Sinhala rendering may be translated into English as follows:
"Sweet and intimate words there were between
them worthy of their good manners
and friendly disposition (to wit) Having

glanced at them, furtively, you have vanquished
the water lilies' blue lustre.
Behold the black geese overjoyed by the pollen
of flowers in the lake that have bloomed in
autumn's splendour."

These renderings, however, fail to give a clear understanding of the sense of the verse or its implied meaning.

The Sigiri damsels and Dame Lake are the best of friends. Sweet words are often exchanged between them in the most cordial and friendly manner. Friend Lake addresses a companion Sigiri damsel as follows:

"You stealthily looked at the lily blooms
and struck them with the blue lustre of your eyes."

It is not that the Sigiri damsel became proud on that account or that she approved or disapproved of the words expressed so lovingly by Dame Lake. Whilst conversing with her friend, vaguely extolling her charms with such refinement, she says something else.

"Look here, at the black geese overjoyed
by the spray of the lake (or by the pollen of the flowers)"

While it is implied that the utterance of Dame Lake that the Sigiri maid by her furtive glance brightens the blue lustre of the lilies in bloom, could be true, it is worth noting how the suggestion is made that the Sigiri maiden's rejoinder embodies the idea that she did look at the overjoyed black geese of the lake in bloom.

"How can the Sigiri maiden abandon such intimate conversation and leave her friend the Lake?."

THE FIVE HUNDRED DAMSELS OF SIGIRIYA

Not everything that greeted the eyes of the poets who visited Sigiriya in the 8th and 9th centuries is extant today. Archaeological excavations reveal that the ravages of time have taken a huge toll. Paintings, ponds, parks and palaces and all other cultural items at Sigiriya have been subject to decay.

That the painted figures on the rock wall themselves suffered much neglect in this process is a fact recorded by the poets. Kit Sanboya says in this verse:

44. නොහි ද කසුන්ගිරිරද් අප සිරිලක් සිහිගිරි පසු
පන්සිය අග්නන් සග යන්නා කෙළෙ පසු
එඩිරුපු දප් බිඳැල(ය්) අ(ත)ළෙ (නැගැ) බෙයද් ආ හිසු
වහසින් (ත)ම මිලියෙන් ඇස කළෙ සි(ට) අග්නන් ම දසු
කි(ත්) ස(ං බො)ායා බද් සතර්පද යි

No-hi da kasun-giri-rad apa Siri-Lak Sihigiri pasu
Pansiya agnan saga yannā keḷe pasu

Eḍi-rupu dap bindala(y) a(ta)ḷe (nägä) beyad ā hisu
Vahasin (ta)ma miliyen äsa kaḷe si(ṭa) agnan ma dasu
K(it) Sa(ṁ -b)oyā bad satar-pada yi

Did not Sihigiri in our Siri-Lak relegate to the background the golden King of Mountains (Meru)? The five hundred damsels retarded (the progress of) him who is going to Heaven. With their gentle smile and the fluttering of their eyelids, the damsels stood here and enslaved me who had come to the summit of the cliff, ascending the lower rocks, after having crushed the pride of insolent foes.

The poet says, he gazed to his heart's content upon five hundred damsels at the top of the rock, while Salabudu in verse 560 gives another description of the five hundred damsels.

560. සිරිලක්දිවැ පිහිටි සිරිබර සිහිගිරී
එ[න මෙ] පතා දනන් මන ගන්නා ගිරි
පන්සියක් අග්නන් නිරිඳු සිකා සිරී
බැලූමො කැටිතල් යහවන් වැ සසිරී

Siri-Lak-divä pihiṭi siribara Sihigirī
E[na me] patā danan mana gannā giri
Pan-siyak agnan nirindu sikā sirī
Bälūmo käṭ-tal yahavan vä sasirī

At Sihigiri, of abundant splendour, situated in the island of Siri-Lak, we saw, in happy mood, the rock which captivates the mind of people who come (here), having longed for this; five hundred damsels who (in their) splendour are (like unto) the crest jewels of the king; and the resplendent mirror- terrace.

Thus for nearly three or four hundred years after the completion of the paintings, Sigiriya abounded with feminine grace. But the five hundred damsels were slowly fading away and disappearing even during this early period. This is implied in the compositions of several poets who addressed the ladies in their graffiti.

Vira –Vidur-bata also refers to 500 paintings of women in the following Stanza:

249. සිහිල් පිනිබිඳින් අද් සවඳ් පවන් [ෙ]ගන මඳ් හමුළෙ
කොඳ් කුමුඳ් වසත්අව්හි මල් සු(සැදි වි) හෙ[බි] මුළුළෙ
තබය් එය් මෙ රන්වනුන් දකුත් මෙ සිත් කාතර කෙළෙ
විදි යමින් මෙ මඳ්බලම්නි වගුළෙමි මෙ ගිරිතෙළෙ
පන්සිය අග්නන් රිසිසෙය් බලය් ගිරිතෙ[ළෙ]
නො ග(නියි ස)ග් මෙනෙ මය් එකක් මෙ (නෙහි)කොට් මනා කොට්

Sihil pini-bindin ad savand pavan g[e]na mand hamuḷe
Kond kumund vasat-avhi mal su(sädi vi) he[bi] muḷuḷe
Tabay ey me ran-vanun dakut me sit kātara keḷe
Vidi yamin me mand-balamni vaguḷemi me giri-teḷe
Pan-siya agnan risi-sey balay giri-te[ḷe]
No ga(niyi sa)g mene may ekak me(nehi) koṭ manā koṭ

The gentle breeze blew-(the breeze) which is wet with cool dew-drops – taking (with it) fragrant perfumes; in the spring sunshine, the jasmine and the water-lily, being adorned with flowers, shone all over. Leaving it (all aside), my mind was agitated on seeing these golden-coloured ones and, being shot at, whilst going, by their side-long glances, I became prostrate on the slope of this rock. Having seen, to my heart's content, the five hundred damsels on the surface of the rock, and having well remembered one (of them), Heaven (itself) does not take my mind.

The poet describes the gentle breeze that blew the cool dew-drops taking with it the fragrant perfume in the spring sunshine. The jasmine and the water-lily plants being adorned with flowers, shone all over. Leaving all this aside, his mind has been agitated whilst going on seeing the golden-coloured ones by their side-long glances, he became prostrate on the slope of this rock.

He has seen, to his heart's content the five hundred damsels on the surface of the rock, and because he remembered well one (of them), Heaven (itself) did not succeed in distracting his mind.

Poet Kith writes, while leaving the rock defeated:

251. පෙරෙ යම් [හැ]ජි[න්] නම් ම පහනිජ් නම් අලලැ
මා එ යත් මෙ එත් නැත පිළි එය්හි සැර්හිමැ
නැතැජ් එ කලු රැතු ගැළ හි හොවින් බිමා
නො කෙල්ලන් වීයින් කියය් අ සි කැරෙය් කිමැ

Pere yam [hä]ji[n] nam ma pahani-j nam alalä
Mā e yat me et näta piḷi eyhi särhimä
Nätä-j e kalu rutu gäḷa hi hovit bimā
No kellan vīyin kiyay a si käre-y kimä

When I go to her whom I knew in former days, and who was gratified in her attachment to me-(when I go to her), these (persons) are coming (from her); there is, again, no adornment in her.Those damsels, though they have no menstrual periods, separate themselves and sleep on the ground, having fallen down there. As they are not young damsels, alas, what will be brought to memory by having told them?.

Paranavitana says that the writer of the verse evidently states that the woman depicted in the painting was his former mistress, but when he was going to her, he met other persons returning from her, and to confirm his suspicions that her love has been transferred elsewhere, she shows no signs of having adorned herself so as to receive him.

Could it be that even as these lines were written, the fallen damsels referred to, be the plaster that was crumbling and falling down in pieces? May be this was how the poet translated reality into poetic imagery.

Another poet, Mahagama Mihind, beautifully transforms the fact of deterioration into poetic motif by saying that it was as if a string of pearls had been loosened, with some pearls still clinging on to the string. This suggests that bits of the plaster in the niche had crumbled and that the figures painted on the rock face were falling off.

325. පෙසෙන වැළැඳුණ සෙය් ගිළිහෙන සෙය් පිරික්සත්
සිලිහි ගිය [මු]ත්වෙළැ මෙ ඇස්හි සිට්මින් බලත්වය්

Pesena väḷänduṇa sey giḷihena sey piriksat
Silihi giya [mu]t-veḷä me äs'hi siṭmin balatvay

When (you) observe the manner in which (they) are attached (to the rock) by a side and the manner in which (they) fall down, may you, standing (here), look at this pearl necklace which has loosened itself and has been scattered about before your eyes.

Of this verse 325 Paranavitana has said:

"This description refers probably to the condition of a painted figure which had become almost completely detached and was clinging by one edge to the rock."

Yet another poet speaks of a damsel playing a lute:

84. ගන රිසි කොට් වයමිනි වෙණ ඔරන් ළග කොට්
නිරිද් ඉසිරා මෙළෙ යි ඈනෑ කඬ නො කළ වෙණ රන්වන්

Gana risi koṭ vayamini veṇa orat ḷaga koṭ
Nirid isirā meḷe yi änä kaṇḍa no kaḷa veṇa ran-van

The golden-coloured one, being desirous of singing, played the lute against her shoulder and was playing it; (but, having heard) that the king (her) lord had died, did she not strike (with it) and reduced the lute into fragments?

No such figure is found today. And considering that the lines were probably written in late Eighth or early Ninth century, we may suspect that the poet was in fact writing about a painting that was already in a visible state of decay.

However, these lines can be interpreted differently. The stanza's meaning rests on the phrase "*kada no kala Vena ana*". Several meanings can be read into these words, for example:

Didn't (She) break the lute by thrusting it onto the ground?
She broke it, didn't she?
(There) she has broken it.

It is also not impossible to give other interpretations such as – after hearing the news of the king's death, didn't she smash the lute on the ground and break it? Or why didn't she do so even after hearing the news of the king's death?

If the word-order is changed to read "*Vena (bima) ana kada kala no*?" the meaning becomes different again. It suggests that she broke the lute by smashing it on the ground. Whatever it is, this goes to show the marvel of poetic imagination concerning the figure of a damsel playing a lute.

Verse19 written by Mahamet and sung by Laya Sivala speaks of another lute player.

19. තනරන්-මලී වෙණ අතනි ගත් හො රන්වන් ලි
නිරිදු මෙළෙන් එකල් නො මෙ බෙ[ණෙය්] අන් නන හය් යාවත්

Tana-ran-malī veṇa atani gat ho ran-van li
Niridu meḷen ekal no me be[ṇey] an nna hay yāvat

She, the golden-coloured damsel, who (wears) a golden chain on her breast and has taken a lute in her hand, does not speak to anyone else whomsoever, as the king died at the time.

She who mourned the death of her king has also vanished from the rock face. A damsel holding a lute is not found among the paintings preserved at Sigiri.

Were all the graffiti about women and their beauty inspired by the figures on the rock face? A careful examination of the actualities behind the poetic fancies leads to the conclusion that stanzas have been composed not only about the painted figures on the rock wall, but also about other women not depicted thereon.

Why would other women be a subject for the songs of the Sigiri poets? The graffiti themselves supply the answer to this question.

Paranavitana observes in 'Sigiri Graffiti' Vol. I, p. ccxv, ..:

"It will be seen that the authors of our verses not only belonged to various stations in social life, but also hailed from places far distant from one another. A question that might arise is whether it was sightseeing alone that drew them to Sigiri. In this connection it may perhaps be not too far-fetched to mention that, in ancient India, the practice prevailed of holding festivities on the summits of rocks. In such festivities, called '*giragga-samajja*' there was much merry-making, dancing, and singing. There may even have been theatrical performances of some sort. Could the writers of our stanzas have visited Sigiri to attend a festival corresponding to the old *giragga-samajja*, probably celebrated annually? The information supplied incidentally by some of our verses, for instance No: 174, that in those days visitors came to Sigiri in large numbers, is not inconsistent with such a surmise.

174. (අ)[වු](ද්) මුළු වෙ ගිරිහි යන වී අප මුළු විසිරි
[සි]හිදුන් සෙය හැඟැ අප සිහි වන්නට් සිහිගිරී

(A)[vu](d) muḷu ve girihi yana vī apa muḷu visiri
[Si]hid=un seya hä(ṅ)gä apa sihi vannaṭ Sihigirī

Having come here, (the people) become crowded (together) on the rock. The lord of lions, it seems, felt (this) and stood here in order that we may scatter ourselves from the crowd and go away, and also to secure that Sihigiri shall be impressed on our memory.

Sigiri stanzas support the historical fact that visitors congregated at the rock either to celebrate an Indian style festival traditionally held on mountain tops or to join similar festive occasions and enjoy themselves to the accompaniment of music and song. It is apparent that among those who participated in these revels, there were beautiful women and ladies of high rank.

Some of the stanzas suggest that the females were eager to draw the men into conversation, exchange love-talk and engage in amorous activities, while the men on their part sought the pleasurable company of women.

Incidents that occurred thus in real life could well have contributed to the poetic background for the graffiti on the Mirror wall.

Evidence supports the view that some of the women who participated in these revelries were bedecked in much feminine finery, and carried bouquets of flowers in their hands as did the painted figures.

Verse number 659, whose author Paranavitana conjectures was using a nom de plume, was definitely not referring to the figure of a damsel. The poet only speaks of a woman who was holding blue water-lilies. But it says'beyandhi hindi' who 'remained on the mountain side' which indicates that it is a fresco.

659. මට හො අත දි යමිනි මනා කොට් ගිය හැක්කැජ්
ම අස්වැසී බෙයන්ද් [හි] න්දි මහනෙල් අති[න් ග]ත්තී

Maṭa ho ata di yamini manä koṭ giya häkkä j
Ma asväsī beyand [hi] ndi mahanel ati[n ga]ttī

She who remained on the mountain side and has taken water-lilies in her hand, consoled me by having given her hand to me while walking, though she is able to walk well (by herself).

The special features in the fashions and the physical gestures seen in the painted figures of the 5th century would without doubt have kindled the interest of the women of the 8th and 9th centuries who joined in the festivities. They would have been encouraged to emulate the hair styles, ornaments, dress and floral arrangements depicted on the rock wall because these were attributes approvingly described by the poets. Such behaviour would have endeared them all the more to the male pleasure-seekers visiting Sigiriya.

While the poets of the day had no necessity to make special mention of the festivities, certain facts pertaining to them seem to have crept into the contents of some verses. The verse (286) composed by Vajur Agboi, a resident in the household of a lady called Satha, is an example.

286. ගල්මුඳුන් නැගී බැලීමි බෙයන්‍ද මා සිත්
රෙපෙ දුන් මගුල් කෙළෙමි සීහිමියා බැලැනි වී

Gal-mundun nägī bälīmi beyandä mā sit
Repe dun magul keḷemi sī-himiyā bäläni vī

I ascended the summit of the rock and looked at (things). On the mountain side I celebrated festivities which (as it were) gave form to my thoughts. All this came to pass through the might of His Majesty the Lion.

Poth Dev notes in verse 356 that he came to Sigiriya carrying food and drink.

356. ජිවෙල් ගෙන යින් මෙ සිරිබර්නි මයි ආ රස
බැලුමො ගුයුන බ[ල] ත් බෙ[ය*]න්‍දිහි රන්වනුන් දුටිමො

Jivel gen=ayin me siri-barni mayi ā rasa
Bälumo guyuna ba[la] t   be[ya*]nd'hi ran-vanun duṭmo

As I came (here) bringing (with me) means of sustenance, delight came (into being) from the abundant splendour of this. We looked at the sky and, when we looked, we saw the golden-coloured ones on the mountain side.

Such direct statements as well as the allusions contained in the descriptions leave no room to doubt that people did assemble at the rock to hold festivities. At such assemblies women attracted the attention of the poets, and the women came to be immortalized in the verses.

In verse 410 written by a poet called Weligama Agbohi it is said that a washerwoman mingled among the crowds on the rock, perhaps because she could not find on top of the rock a waterhole and the paraphernalia needed for washing clothes. Her presence there may have outraged the poet. It could even be that this woman was known to the poet. This indicates the probability that the poets freely used the graffiti to write not only about the painted figures of damsels, but also about the women who participated in the festivities.

410. පිළ අපුලන තොට් නැත්තෙන් හළුගර් නැත්තෙන්
වැ[ද] වෙසෙය් රිදියක් බෙයන්‍දිහි රන්වනුන් අතුරෙ

Piḷa apulana toṭ nätten haḷugar nätten
Vä[dä] vesey ridiyak beyan'hi ran-vanun ature

As there is no piece of water where clothes are washed and as there is no clothes-house, a washer woman has gone into the midst of the golden coloured ones on the mountain side and remains there.

A verse (382) sung by Samana Himi who deals with the women who congregated at the rock.

382. මෙයට එන මදනල වල්විජ්නා සියලෙලනි
සෙයි මෙ අය් (ග)ත ලියයුන ග(ල්)බෙයදආ මු(දුන)ට

Meyaṭa ena mada-nala val-vijnā siyalleni
Seyi me ay (ga)ta liyayuna ga(l)-beyada ā mu(duna)ṭa

The gentle breeze which came to this (place) is as if it came from all the (yak)-tail fans taken (in their hands) by the ladies who have come to the top of this precipitous rock.

Among the large number of women who visited Sigiriya there were some who carried fans and whisks. They fanned themselves to get over their fatigue. For the poet, the gentle breeze that swept over Sigiriya originated in the graceful hands of the women fanning themselves. If we consider the fact there are no fan-bearing maidens in the paintings, it is reasonable to assume that these lines were written not about the painted figures but about the actual women who were visiting Sigiriya.

Verse 393 reveals information that could in no way be explained in terms of the extant paintings.

393. කරය් ලබු පෙ[රෙ]ට් පියහට් ගැඬැව් සඳ්හය
තොමො ඔ සැ[දී] අ ගමන් ම හජත් එල්බ මල්කඩ ගත

Karay labu pe[re]ṭ piyahaṭ gändäv sand'haya
T[o]m[o] o sä[dī] a gaman ma hajat elba mal-kaḍa gata

Holding a flowering branch in front (of her), she, having adorned herself, came walking forward for the purpose of (providing) music to (her) lover; (but) when I attract her, (she), having bent forward, accepted (from me) the spray of flowers.

"A woman came forward to play music for her lover". Upon seeing her, the poet walked up to her and managed to attract her attention. He moreover succeeded in making her accept the bouquet of flowers he offered her.

The next two verses (Nos. 394 and 395) seem to have been written by the same hand, although, as Paranavitana has surmised, they could have been composed by two persons who had come from the same place although committed to writing by one.

394. බඳු බැ[මැ] නිම්පතෙක්හි [සඳ්] හය් එක් වනා
එමු පැරැයු ළඳුරිය තොල්හි ළ[ප]ලුන[ා]
ළගොබ්පතක් බඳු මහනෙල් ලමු කරනා
ම හය් කල් යෙහෙළි කි දිග අත්(සලමි)නා

Bandu bä[mä] nim-patek'hi [sand] hay ek vanā
E-mu päräyu ḷa-däriya tolhi ḷa-[pa]lu n[ā]
Ḷa-gob-patak bandu mahanel lamu karanā
Ma hay kal yeheḷi k[i] diga at (salami)nā

395. හැමැ ජෙනෙ රන්වනුන් දුට්[මො] යි බොරු කියති [බ](ස්)
(හෙ) නො කියැ හෙය්නි සොව් කොට් හිරි වැ[ටි] බෙවින් [නො] බසි [යි] වය්

Hämä jene ran-vanun duṭ[mo] yi boru kiyati [ba](s)
(He) no kiyä heyni sov koṭ hiri vä[ṭi] bevin (no) basi[yi] vay

The first verse is by a monk named Kayabure Sen. It goes like this:

'(Her) eyebrow is like a leaf of the nim (tree), her face resembles the moon; by the lips of the young maiden the tender leaves of the na tree have been worsted'. So said to me, waving her long arms, the charming confidante, who is like unto a tender leaf and who holds down (in her hand) a water-lily.

The second verse is by Kayabure Sivu. It goes like this:

'We saw the golden coloured ones', thus everyone
utters false words. He, being unable to tell (lies), has
come to grief and, as he is ashamed, does not indeed come down.

While the two poets were promenading, and viewing the paintings, they met a female acquaintance. She was very beautiful, pleasant and young. She was holding a lily in her hand. This comely attractive girl who was looking at one of the frescoes turned to the poet and expressed her opinion about the painting. It is this incident that was the subject of the verse.

This verse has a special significance in that the poet's description compliments the beauty of the painting and the living lady. Usually, the poets focus upon the flowers in the hands of the Sigiriya damsels. In this instance, the visitor too carries water-lilies. She is moved by the beauty of the paintings and speaks of faces, lips and eyebrows. The poet in turn expresses his admiration of her physical charms. Visitor and painting are equally attractive. This poetic fancy would have derived from a real-life experience.

Similarly, verse 399 clearly was not written about any figure of a damsel. The poet here employs '*ranavana*', a word repeatedly used by poets, with a satiric intention.

399. වහවත වහවමහ [මෙ]සෙයනි අ[ප] සිති වියි[න]
[නො] රෙන්දෙ වෙනෙ සිනපට බෙජි [එ] රනවන [මෙ] පිළිසනට

Vahavata vahavamaha [me]-seyani a[pa] siti viyi[na]
[No]-rende vene sina-paṭa beji [e] rana-vana [me] piḷisanaṭa

If we bear (ourselves) up, we do so as it has been thought by us in this wise: 'That golden-coloured one, who has used Chinese silk (in her attire), will not remain herself in this forest for the sake of concealment.

This verse could be interpreted in several ways. The poet is so enamoured of the lady that he is totally distracted by her. He can console himself only with the thought that the lady, so richly attired and used to a life of luxury had not come to dwell among the trees. Whatever her purpose, she could leave the forest in the poet's company.

Another interpretation is that the gold-coloured lady has not come to hide in the forest. If so, why is she lingering? Is she waiting for a man like the poet?

The poetic merit of the stanza stems from such ambiguities. The verse can also be read as follows: People visit Sigiriya to see the golden-damsels. They are found in the rock cave and on the face of the rock. This too is a golden hued damsel; but she does not dwell in the rock cave. She is in the forest; her clothes are different. Unlike the Sigiriya damsels, she wears rich silken dresses.

A woman named Dayal writes a verse (392) not about the painted damsels, but about herself.

392. වල්විජ්නා පෙරෙට් මිණි පැය් දිග්ඇස්සක්
ගත් අතැ රන් සොලුයෙක් තොමො ලීය් මෙ රන්දම් පැලැන්දී

Val-vijnā pereṭ miṇi päy dig-ässak
Gat atä ran soluyek tomo līy me ran-dam pälāndī.

A long-eyed one who exhibited, as it were, jewels in front of a yak-tail fan, and who, in her hand, has taken a golden-staff - (she) herself, who is adorned with a golden chain, wrote this.

Paranavitana is of the opinion that the fan here is her lock of hair, and the gems her eyes.

Poet Kottha has also written verse 299, about the eyes of a woman whom he encountered at the summit of the rock.

299. නැගි සිසි සඳ බලය් බසි[ත] සඳ්හන කොට [ම]න
නෙ[ත්] නිල් මී[ලැස්න] පිළිදීජොත්ත සිහි විනි

Nägi sisi sanda balay bas[ita] sand'hana koṭa [ma]na
Ne[t] nil mī[läsna] piḷi-d[ī] jotta [s]ihi v[i]n[i]

When (I) climb down, having looked at (this) when the moon had arisen, and having kept in my mind the blue eyes of the deer-eyed ones, the light of a crystal lamp came to my mind.

The poet, having gazed upon the women assembled at the top of the mountain, climbs down to the Mirror Wall to write a verse. He still remembers the beauty of the woman's eyes. The attractive blue eyes, their light combining with the streaks of moon beams, conjure up the image of a lamp made of white crystal. It is clear that this verse does not deal with any of the painted figures.

The pleasure derived from the company of women was not second to that brought about by the sight of the painted figures. Poets descending from the top of the mountain, still dazzled by the memory of the beautiful women they had seen, may have lost sight of the painted figures. "I had the pleasure of watching women at the summit of the rock" could be explained in this light.

435. අ[වුද් නැගි] මෙ බෙයද් සිත් සෙ බැලිමි දි [ගැස්ස]න්
තොස කතු[න්] බලත ලදිමි (සිටි) [සිහිගිරි ග]ල [මත]

A[vud nägi] me beyad sit se bälimi di[gässa]n
Tosa katu[n] balata ladimi (siṭi) [Sihigiri ga]la [mata]

Having come and ascended the mountain side, I looked at the long-eyed ones to my heart's content. When I looked at the damsels who stand on the summit of the Sihigiri rock, I obtained pleasure.

Sigiriya poets made various references to damsels who appeared to honour a vow of silence and never opened their lips. But one visitor speaks of golden-hued ones with their voices intact. When the poet says my eyes were drawn to them, he conveys to the reader the pleasurable sensation he received.

438. බෙ[ය]ඳ්හි මෙ දුට්වෙන් රන්වනුන් [සි]ටි බස් ඇති
නෙත් දෙක දිවි යනු බඳු වි සෙ රන්වනුන් සිටි බල

Be[ya]nd'hi me duṭven ran-vanun [si]ṭi bas äti
Net deka divi yanu bandu vi se ran-vanun siṭi bala

As (I) saw golden-coloured ones who are endowed with speech and who stood on this mountain side, the two eye (of mine), as it were, went (out to them), running of their own accord. (You, too), look at the manner in which the golden-coloured ones stood.

Mihidal alludes to the females who visited the rock as well as to those that were painted on the Wall:

441. ලැබු මෙ සි වී නො මඳ් හි[ම බු]න් බලත ඇති වන්
මන මෙන් බෙ(යඳ් මෙ නැගි) අව රන්(වනුන් අතුරෙ)

Läbu me si vī no mand hi[mabu]n balata äti van
Mana men be(yand me nägī) ava ran(vanun ature)

When, having ascended this mountain side in accordance with my mind, I am come in the midst of the golden-coloured ones, is not this smile, received when looking at the ladies as they are, enough ?

The poet climbed the mountain. He walked past the painted ones without receiving so much as a smile. Then he came among the "live ones" at the summit. The poet was overjoyed by looking at them, and is rewarded with a smile. This makes him happy.

Poet Agal Bati, a resident of the Northern Province says:

450. (බෙයඥිහි රන්වනුන් මය් දස බලය් නුයුනින්
මහනෙල් ගත් අතිනි බෙණෙත් සෙළෙන් අයුන් හය්)
සෙළෙන් අ [බැ]ඥි මෙයට් බෙයඥිහි වන්දබුයුන්
නිරිඥු මළ නො මළ එ ගැහැනින් අසදහ යත් කි වරජ්

(Beyandihi ran-vanun may dasa balay nuyunin
Mahanel gat atini beṇet seḷen ayun hay)
Seḷen a [bä]ndi meyaṭ beyandihi vandabuyun
Nirindu maḷa no maḷa e gähänin asadaha yat ki varaj

The golden-coloured ones on the mountain side, having looked at me with their eyes, speak deceitfully, by means of (their) hands which bear water-lilies, with those who have come (here).

The widowed ones on the mountain side deceitfully captivated those who came to this. What fault is there if one were to say that those women are faithless ones;(they) who did not die when the king died?

Were both these verses written about the painted figures? The first alludes to the golden-hued damsels of the cave; the second, to the gold coloured ones who had come to the cave. It is possible to conjecture that the two poetic expressions speak of visitors as well as of the inanimate figures. For there is an implied meaning in these lines. Literally, they mean:

I. The gold-coloured damsels of the cave glance at me and then exchange confidences with others carrying flowers.

II. The widowed damsels of the cave have deceptively enticed the visitors. So is it wrong to suspect the moral values of women who did not die along with their lord? Does not this sentiment correspond with the conventional truism that "all women are prone to deceitful behaviour?" The character attributes of the visiting females and of those painted on the wall are the same, the poet hints. The women visitors glance secretively at one person and speak surreptitiously with another. These widowed women of the rock cave tempted the visitors and captivated them. They were unconcerned about the king's death. Can readers be blamed for taking this particular sense to be part of the poet's intention?

Much evidence can be adduced from the graffiti to demonstrate that visiting poets did not confine their attention to the painted figures alone.

That they sought the company of the females who congregated there, and enjoyed conversing with them is a strong possibility that emerges from their verses.

A conversation that took place between two friends who visited Sigiriya is translated into poetic idiom in verse 618:

618. බෙයඳ් නැගි එ ම කී කත තමා හය් එයී
ගිය හො ත් සිහිගිරි මත ත නො ගන්නි සිත [සි*] හිගිරි

Beyand nägi e ma kī kata tamā hay eyī
Giya hot Sihigiri mata ta no ganni sita [Si *]higiri

If (you) were to go to the summit of Sihigiri, (thinking) that the damsel who had ascended the mountain side, and of whom I spoke, will come with you, Sihigiri will not captivate your mind.

This verse is built around an incident concerning two friends and a lady whom they met at Sigiriya. One friend tells the other that Sigiriya would have no attraction for him if his mind was distracted by visiting females of her kind.

Kamal Bata, author of verse 571, is a veritable misogynist. Far from becoming a slave to the beauty of living women he even desists from viewing the golden-hued ones of the paintings.

571. බෙයද් බලය් දිගැසි අර ගැති තබයි ව[නු ම]යි
මෙ වෙත[හි] නො [ය]මි ලයි බෙයදහි රන්වනුන් වැන්නන්

Beyad balay digäsi ara gäti tabayi va[nu ma]yi
Me veta[hi] no [ya]mi layi   beyadahi ran-vanun vännan

Leaving (aside) my becoming a slave to that long-eyed one, (by) having looked at the mountain side, I shall not (even) go to the vicinity of persons like these golden-coloured ones on the mountain-side.

Here the poet is literally pointing his finger at a woman who had come to visit Sigiriya. Is there some tension between him and her? A painting could hardly have brought forth such a state of feeling.

A close examination of the poetic material confirms the view that the writers of graffiti drew inspiration not only from the golden-hued damsels of the paintings but also from the appearance and behaviour of the pleasure-seeking ladies who visited Sigiriya.

VIVIFICATION OF SONG THROUGH DIALOGUE

The Sigiri poets employed a variety of devices to express imaginatively their poetic feelings. Of the many devices so employed to express their poetic sentiments the brilliance of which was enhanced by their creative genius and imagination, the figure of speech known as dialogue (*uba-bas-lakara*) occupies a special place. The poets' ideas and feelings which took the form of "woven textures" (*gettam*) on the mirror wall were always expressed in accordance with the norms of contemporary poetical theory.

The fact that the fair ladies serve as the focus of attention was a factor that determined the poets' choice of dialogue (*uba-bas*) as a mode of literary expression. Some poets evidently preferred engaging in a pleasant conversation with the maidens to indulging in the exercise of composing verses in their presence. They wished to put questions to them, and to get their answers. In such a context, dialogue was the appropriate poetic device. The poets were thus able to rid themselves of the monotony of the conventional literary modes and infuse a lively quality to their poems.

The figure of speech, which received the approbation of the Sigiriya poet, was used by him in diverse ways. In one verse the poet addresses the damsels and they reply. In another, the damsels address the poet and he replies. The poet engages in a light conversation with a friend, himself a poet. A Sigiri damsel engages in a conversation with a female friend. Thus the same dialogue method appears in different forms.

Senarat Paranavitana observes that the dialogue figure of speech (*ubabas*) is not recognized as a poetic figure in Sanskrit poetic theory and that it received due recognition as a literary figure in Sinhala.

"The term *ubabas* used in the *Sidat Sangarava* for dialogue cannot be traced back to any poetic figure used in Sanskrit."

It should be noted also that Gate Mudaliyar W.F.Gunawardhana in p. viii of his *Guttila Kavya Varnanava* states that it is needless to say that "*Ubhaya bhasa laksana*" (the dialogue feature) is distinct from the feature of *Vakrokti* the figure of indirect expression.

Numerous instances can be cited to show that this figure which does not occur in Sanskrit poetics but is found in Sinhalese poetics, received the enthusiastic approval of classical writers and continues to be popular among contemporary writers as well.

There is enough evidence to show that the dialogue figure exercised a special fascination on sensitive minds during the time the *Sidat Sangarava* was written.

උතුරු පසතුරු දෙන
දෙදෙනකු වදන් පිරියතැ
වැනියම් සිරිත් වෙසෙසක්
පළවතුබබස් නම් වේ. (12.10)

"If, at the end of a conversation between two (persons) which takes the form of question and answer, a special character trait that is sought to be expressed, is elicited, it is the (figure of speech) dialogue (*ubabas*)."

In such terms does the *Sidat Sangarava* author define the dialogue figure. Whatever be the case in Sanskrit literature, this figure of speech has been a favourite mode of literary expression not only in our verse literature but in our prose writing too. The folk poet living in the remotest village, be he a singer of songs of the watch-hut, a cart, a mine or a boat has availed himself of the dialogue figure. It must be because of the sympathetic response of sensitive minds that an important place has been accorded to the dialogue figure in such poems as *Kav Silumina*, the finest flower of Sinhala poetry based on the Sanskrit poetic tradition, *Parakumba Sirita*, *Guttila Kavyaya* and *Buduguna Alankaraya* of the Kotte period. This however is not the place for detailed discussion of them.

The extent of the dialogue's popularity among contemporary men of taste (*rasika*) is reflected in (the verses of) the mirror wall.

Let us examine a few Sigiri verses with a view to understanding the thought processes of the Sigiri poet.

The song of Aboyi Dalamaya, son of Mihindala mal of Talaboya, is a dialogue between the poet and the Sigiri maidens.

626. තලබොය මි [හිඳ]ලමලුන් පුත් අබොයි ද[ළ]මෙයිම් මය ගී
මහනෙල්වනින් එ ක දටය මෙ මෙ හෙළිල්ලබු යෙ
තොප මෙනෙහි පුලුද් මෙ නෙ වි යි අ [ග]න නො කා කොට් දිට

Talaboya Mi[hinda]la-malun put Aboyi Da[ḷa]meyimi mayi gī
Mahanel-vanin e ka daṭaya me me helillabu ye
Topa menehi pulud me ne vi yi a[ṅga]na no kā koṭ diṭa

'O lily-coloured ones, when he has seen whom does (he) say that this one, indeed, is the fair damsel?' "This one is not attached (to me)", so (thinking), in the 0manner of whom has not the woman been seen in your mind?'

Addressing the females, the Sigiri poet inquires: 'O lily-coloured ones, seeing (you), he asks, who the fair damsel is. (He asks who indeed is the fair damsel. This is how the poet says, by implication, that the fair one was present there).

It is not surprising for a person who realizes that a young girl does not return his love to see her faults. The reply which the young man who asked "which girl indeed was lovely?" got from the young damsel of Sigiriya was an indirect suggestion that when it is stated that the girl is not lovely what is really meant is that the girl had no feelings of love towards the poet but that she gave vent to her anger.

The following is a dialogue between the poet Dala Meyi and another poet:

622. [ඔ]යුන සිවි එ ම [දෙ]සෙ සිතෙ වි කෙසෙ ද [ම]න් ත නැත
[ම]න් නැතෙයින් [මෙ]හි අව දිගැස්[ස]න් ම දෙසෙ සි[වි]

[O]yuna sivi e ma [de]se site vi kese da [ma]n ta näta
[Ma]n nätteyin [me]hi ava digäs[sa]n ma dese si[vi]

' "That smile of theirs is in my direction." How has (this) been in (your) mind if there be no self-conceit in you?' 'The long-eyed ones smiled with me in my direction when I come (here), as there is no self-conceit (in me).'

"Their smile comes my way"(They smile with me). If you had no self-conceit, how does such a thought (as this) arise?

It is because I had no self-conceit that the long-eyed ones smiled at me.

The following dialogue in a lighter vein, between the poet and his friend if re-constructed in the colloquial idiom of the present day would take a form somewhat as follows:

"How conceited you must really be to say that a Sigiri damsel smiled with you?"

The other replies

"When I came here I lost my pride. Since I was no longer proud, the Sigiri damsels smiled with me".

Verse 572 conveys a similar idea

රැඳි බලත සිත් [මය් නෙ] ති[න්]වෙතෙ කැඳැවී කත
බැලි වි ද මෙ තා නෙතකින් දෙව[සරන්] මෙන් හිඳි[යන්]

Rändi balata sit [may ne]ti[n] vete kändavī kata
Bäli vi da me tā netakin dev=a[saran] men hindi[yan]

'When my mind being rejoiced, I am looking at (her), the lovely woman has beckoned to me with her eye to (her) side.' 'Did they, who remained like heavenly nymphs, indeed, look at you with the eye?'

In this verse the poet says this regarding a Sigiri damsel:

"When my mind was fixed on her I was looking at her (in her direction) the fair one beckoned to me with the eye".

A friend who heard those words replies in this strain:

"Did they who resembled heavenly nymphs really look at you with their eyes?"

While the surface meaning here is that the nymph did look at him, the implied insinuation is that she did not really look at him. Such verbal ambiguity and wit are found abundantly in common speech even today.

The literary figure of dialogue fosters the growth and development of such modes of speech.

The poet Mihindala of the house of Mahasiva Madabi, puts the following question to Sigiri damsels:

'Friend, did not the deceased (King Kasub) in former times (say or) do anything with you?'

The Sigiri ladies reply and their words make the poet speechless.

570. සිකි තොප හය පෙරෙ කිසි ද නො කළහු මළහු
කළහු සමු දිනි තොප හය මළ ඔයුහු නො බ[ණන] සෙ[යි]

Siki topa haya pere kisi da no kaḷahu maḷahu
Kaḷahu samu dini topa haya maḷa oyuhu no ba[ṇana] se[yi]

'My dear, did he who is dead not do anything with you?' 'He did; he gave order so as not to speak with you when he is dead'.

The verse which Tambagolu Kiti of the house of Siddat Madabi wrote, conveys an experience that we may encounter even today.

When one has chosen to remain in the shade and see Sigiriya rather than ascend the hill and expose himself to the heat of the sun, he is derided in fun by another visitor who says: 'Having come to see Sigiriya, you have, it appears, opted to rest in the shade without exposing yourself to the sun,' the former replies: 'Do not bother about my faults, go and see the Sigiri damsels.' In that reply is encapsulated an experience that one may encounter in contemporary society.

391. මෙහි බිම අවු නොසිටි එති නො බැලුමො යි සිහිගිරි
බෙයදැහි රන්වනුන් දකු මෙ හි ම නො සඳ්හන් වැ [දො]ස

Mehi bima avu no-siṭi eti no bälumo yi Sihigiri
Beyadahi ran-vanun daku me hi ma no sand'han vä [do]sa

'Do they not come to the ground here, where the sunshine does not remain, saying "We looked at Sihigiri"?' 'See the golden-coloured ones on the mountain side without having my faults remembered.'

To the one who rests in the shade the poet says: 'You say you've seen Sigiriya and come down here to remain in the shade.' To which the other remaining in the shade replies, in the above strain.

A sensitive soul (*rasika*) looking at the Sigiri ladies was warned by another visitor. Thereafter a conversation ensues between them.

523. [නො] බල [මෙ]ය බලතුජ් නො වී මට් අස්වැසිලී
කිම මෙ[හි] ආ නො ජැනැ තා ගලැ කළ තද් ළ [ඇ]ත්[තී]

[No] bala [me]ya balat=uj no vī maṭ asväsilī
Kima me[hi] ā no jänä tā galä kaḷa tad ḷa [ä]t[tī]

Look not at this. Even when (I was) looking at (this), there was no consolation for me. You come here, not having known that she is one who has a heart as hard as if it were made of stone. Is it not (so)?.

Not knowing that she has a hard heart as if it were made of stone you came here, did you not?

In this manner, the first visitor admonishes his friend not to look at the ladies. However long you keep looking at them, you will have no consolation from them, no solace whatever. Will you have a word or a smile from them or at least, even a loving glance? Thus, they give no comfort was the first one's warning.

The other's rejoinder implies that one should not expect too much from them. That is why he asks the former whether he has come there without even knowing that they have hard hearts as if they were made of stone. Should one really come to those women for comfort?

Poet Budal the Clerk who has climbed Sigiriya keeps on looking at the Sigiri damsels for a long time. But they do not engage in any conversation with him. They do not even smile. Nor do they even recognise him.

527.

ම ලද රන්ව[නු]න් ගලැ බලන්නෙ
බණත් කිය(නෙය) සැනෙක හැරැ යනෙ
එ ද නැත බණන මැය සැබැවිනෙ
පවෙහි ආ [෧]කනෙක් මතු මෙ ජනනෙ

Ma lada ran-va[nu]n galä balanne
Baṇat kiya(neya) säneka hārä yane
E da näta baṇana mäya säbävine
Pavehi ā k[e]nek matu me janane

Look at the golden-coloured ones obtained by me on the rock! Were they to speak, (they) would say: 'Leave (me) and go (away) in an instant' There is not, in fact, even that (much of) speaking in this (damsel). This should be known by any one (who would) come to this rock in the future.

Finally the poet says:

"If you do not speak to us, why do you not at least ask us to go away?"

The fancied reply of the maidens is a clever one. It is a reply that every one should understand according to his or her own capacity. It might please a poet, or it might displease him. That depends on the interpretation one gives of it. And that is because it is the outcome of feminine wit.

The reply of the damsels was:

"We saw the route by which you reached Sigiriya. How did you arrive here?"

One who considers that it was a sympathetic response may interpret it as follows:

"We were watching the route by which you came to Sigiriya. It is a difficult one. Did you not take that difficult route to see us? How good of you. How did you come through such a difficult route? It is because we were thinking of that that we could not speak".

The damsels' reply can also be given another interpretation.

'We were watching the route you took to come up here. It remains the same as it was. By the same route as you took to come here, and in the same manner, you may return. Even as you did not need our permission to come here, why do you need our permission to return?'

That was how they said that he could return the same way as he came by, without explicitly stating so.

Another verse embodying a conversation is the following:

295. කි[ම නො] කියහි යා යි තකුද් ආ මි[හි ද]ස්නට්
මොබ ආ තුප කෙසෙ බැලු මො [නැ] ග ආ මග සිහිගිරි

Ki[ma no] kiyahi yā yi tak=ud ā mi[hi da]snaṭ
Moba ā tupa kese bälumo [nä] ga ā maga Sihigirī

'Wherefore do you not say even as much as "Go" to (your) slaves who are come (here)?' 'We looked at the road (by which) you climbed and came to Sihigiri, (wondering) how you came here'.

Verse 476 may be reckoned as one that reveals the attitudes of two poets towards the long-eyed damsels and the lion's figure at Sigiriya.

476. [දි]ගැ[ස්] ගිරිහිසැ හිඳි ඇවිද් මෙ ග[ල] බැලුමෙ
[බ]ලමනා තක් ඇවි[ද්] බැලුමො සී සිහිගිරි

[Di]gä[s] giri-hisä hindi ävid me ga[la] bälumo
[Ba]lamanā tak ävi[d] bälumo sī Sihigirī

'Having come to this rock, we looked at the long-eyed one who remained on the summit of the rock.' 'We came and looked at the Lion of Sihigiri – all that is worth looking at.'

"We came to the rock and saw the long-eyed ones", says one. The other replies: "What is really worth seeing at Sigiriya, the lion, we saw".

Though couched in the form of a dialogue, these ideas are expressed by one and the same poet. The mode of expression the poet has employed here stresses the fact that, as a work of creative art the figure of lion surpassed the figures of the Sigiri damsels and it merits the consideration of the critic of good taste (*sahrdaya*). *Sahṛdaya* like *rasika* referred to earlier is a term which presents difficulties to writers in English. This term, even more than *rasika* draws attention to the aesthetic experience of the reader or the poet. Literally the word means one who has a heart, i.e. one who is capable of feeling and who has the capacity to enjoy an aesthetic experience (poem, drama etc.). It may thus refer to the poet in his capacity of creative artist, or to the reader in his capacity as one who enjoys the aesthetic experience.

The song composed by the poet Jet (245) and the one composed by the poet Kitdev (246), though not directly revealing features of a dialogue, demonstrate a more important trait. Those two stanzas provide firm evidence of poetical competitions that apparently occurred among poets who came to see the damsels of Sigiriya.

The verse composed by the contestant Jet is the following:

245. සෙනෙහින් ළැගු කසුබ් කලු පියය් ඇ[විද්] මය්
ගිඅතුරෙ පෙලෙබි කුමට් යගී මෙහි ලියන්නෙය්

Senehin ḷägu Kasub kalu piyay ä[vid] may
Gi-ature pelebi kumat yagī mehi liyanney

Having come away discarding the damsels whom Kasub, through love, set up on high, yagi (verses) be written here, among (other) verses, by me having become allured (of them)? I defeated (my opponent) and went away.

"I defeated (my opponent) and went away." This poet who says he has defeated his rival, states, that all the poets who wrote these verses were not inspired by a single motive: That was to win the hearts of the fair ones. With whatever intention the poets wrote their verses, that intention appears to have been realised by poet Jet who wrote this verse. That is why he brags 'Why should I come here and compose *yagi* ?'

Kit-dev who admits he has been defeated in the context writes this verse:

246. දැකැජ් තොප සුනිල් මහනෙල්කැලුම් බැල්මක්
නොයයහන මිනිසුන් කුමට් යගී මෙහි ලියන්නෙය්

Däkä-j topa sunil mahanel-kälum bälmak
No-yayahana minisun kumaṭ yagī mehi liyanney

Why should yagi verses be written here by men who are not able to go (away), even (after) having receiving a glance from you – (a glance which is equal to) the beautifully blue radiance of the lotus flower?

Why should they remain here even after receiving your glance which was matched by the lily's deep "blue luster", to write *yagi* ? Having had but one glance, they are incapable of leaving the place.

It is difficult to imagine what the fate of those who were so enticed by a mere glance from those women would have been had they expected something more. The lustre of their deep blue eyes had rendered them incapable of leaving (the place). There is no point in writing *yagi* with the object of winning them over, confesses the poet Kit-dev when about to leave.

Paranavitana has this to say regarding this pair of verses.

"Verses in graffiti No. 245 and 246, (given above) the results of a competition in composing poems, also serve to illustrate the importance attached by these versifiers to good taste. The first of these two is coarse in sentiment, whereas the second, that which bore away the palm, on the other hand, is most delicate in feeling and expression: (Sigiri Graffiti Vol. I p. CXCIX)

What is meant by the statement that those verses are the result of a poetical contest is not that they were written for the contest, but that they were the final outcome of the contest. Since the winner Jet states that he went away after defeating his rival it is clear that this verse was written after the contest was over and he had been declared the winner.

It is quite evident that the other verse written by the defeated contestant Kit-dev was written by him after his defeat and when he was on the point of leaving the scene.

We are not fortunate enough to have the opportunity of reading the verses which the two poets wrote during the contest.

Of the two verses the one composed by Kit-dev comes in for praise from Paranavitana. It has to be conceded that Jet's verse too is full of implied meaning (*vyangy-ãrtha*).

The verse of Sagal, Private Secretary of Prince Kasabal (Kasabal Apanan ge Payamul Leydaru) is specially important among those composed in the form of a conversation between the poets and the damsels.

320. දෙවියනි මෙවැනි එක සුකක් ඇති කරනු
දෙඅත් වටැ පළ මය් රු සුක රුකුරුවනු
තොල් (ජැ)හැ (යනු) කොට් මිඳිබිය කුරුර වනු
බොටුමල් බලය් සුකනු තය් යහපත් වනු

Deviyani me-väni eka sukak äti karanu
De-at vaṭä paḷa may ru suka rukuruvanu
Tol [jä]hä (yanu) koṭ mindibiya kurura vanu
Boṭu-mal balay sukanu tay yaha-pat vanu

'O gods, do cause some pleasure to arise with one like this.' 'Make my beauty, manifested round about the two hands, (your) pleasure.' 'Having made me go away forsaking (her) lips, the disdainful one has become cruel.' 'Look at the flowers on (my) neck and enjoy pleasure (therefrom). May you become happy.'

The poet who is inflamed with passion after seeing the damsels implores the gods to grant him an opportunity of having sexual gratification with them.

The poet censures the women for having denied him the opportunity of kissing their lips and takes them to task for being so cruel.

What is embodied is a praiseworthy attempt on the part of the damsels to explain to the infatuated poet , the actual circumstances of the case with restraint and gentleness in soft and comforting words: "Far better enjoy the eternal beauty enshrined in them than yearn for casual satisfaction with them," the damsels explain unobtrusively. And finally they wish him well.

The poetic figure of dialogue (*Ubabas lakara*), which does not occur in Sanskrit poetic theory that has exerted such a strong influence on our indigenous theory of poetry, may thus be described as a literary device that bears witness to the identity and individuality of Sinhala poetic practice. It is also a device that enhances the literary quality of the Sigiri verses by imparting to them the qualities of vigour and freshness.

NECTAR OF SONG

The Sigiri Paintings and the Poets

The *ranvanun* and *nilvanun* (gold-hued ones and blue-tinted ones) of the Sigiriya paintings form an Art gallery of major significance in the history of Sri Lanka's cultural milieu. Historians, epigraphists, archaeologists and art-critics dispute the identity and symbolism of these female figures: they have been seen as cloud maidens, lightning princesses, heavenly beings, noblewomen, ladies of the harem and consorts of Avalokitesvara; they are seen as floating in clouds, as on the way to water sports, as bearing flowers to a pooja, as mourning, as contemplating suicide on the death of their Lord, as arriving from Tusita heaven.

But the poets have shown us a different way of viewing the paintings. Of the thousands who have visited Sigiriya, some have expressed their responses in poems inscribed on the Mirror Wall that runs parallel to the paintings. It is as if their voices can be heard as we experience the delicacy of their thought and the variety of their responses; the feelings, thoughts, customs and manners of a people encoded in the poem are, using the resources of the contemporary language; The names and titles of the writers suggest the wide diffusion of poetic culture: the writers include kings, noblemen, ladies, monks, a novice, a guard, a smith (the last giving us one of the most moving of the poems).

Several of the visitors speculate like the historians and archaeologists on the identity of the ladies of the paintings: they, too, see them as apsaras, as consorts, mourning, or on their way to a pooja. But the majority teach us a different way to appreciate them: seeing them as ideal representations of the feminine, they respond to their beauty, their allure, their mystery. One poet sees a lady as enticing, with lovely breasts, another says "Although she doesn't favour me with her love, just seeing such a beauty is enough for me (rejoices me)." Sometimes the response is openly sensual:

My body is thrilled by you, its hair
stiffening with desire.

Sometimes it is brutally cynical: basing himself on the conceit that the ladies are at the rock face to throw themselves down in their bereavement, one poet wonders why they don't go ahead and do it.

But the finest poems convey subtle shades of response to the paintings; fully alive to their sensuous beauty, the poets also read them in terms of suggestion, metaphor and symbol while themselves making delicate and creative uses of suggestion or tone and poetic form.

Thus several of the poems explore the language of flowers. For the flowers in the hands of the Sigiri damsels are seen as eloquently expressive, though the paintings themselves are, of course, silent. Poet Sivala of Hedigam in his song imagines a lady confessing:

439. අප මන ජ[තුන් සෙය් ඔ] යුන අ වියි මලනි තම
සෙ ඇ[ති] හෙළි විනි [බැ]ලිමි බිතු වසන්නට මෙසෙ ගත

Apa mana ja[tun sey o]yuna a viyi malani tama
Se ä[ti] heḷi vini [bä]limi bitu vasannaṭa mese gata

'Ah! What is in our minds has, it seems, been known by them by means of our flowers.' 'When the wall, in this manner, has been taken (by you) to reside (on), I saw the manner in which what is (in your minds) has been revealed.'

While another is maddened by the suggestions of love conveyed by "the flowers in the hands of the long-eyed ones." Yet another is not offended that a "deer-eyed one" will not look at him, for he is convinced that the blue lotuses in her rosy hands are a promise of love.

655. බෙයන්ද් හින්දි මිලැ[සි] වී දුට් නොජත්තන් සෙය්
රතත් [නි]ලුපුල ම[ල් ග]ත් [වී]යින් අපට් තොස් දිනි

Beyand hindi mīlä[si] vī duṭ no-jattan sey
Rat=at [ni]l=upula ma[l ga]t [vī]yin apaṭ tos dini

The deer-eyed one, who remained on the mountain side, as if she has not recognized (us) (even though) having seen (us), gave pleasure to us as she has taken blue lotus flowers in (her) rosy hand.

To another poet, it is the eyes that speak: 'they give no other speech but glances from their motionless eyes.' Another, on the other hand, regrets that he has not performed enough meritorious deeds in previous births to deserve a glance from eyes like blue lotuses. To many, of course, the silence of these alluring beauties "means" that their hearts have turned to stone in their grief over the death of the King.

Some poets are led by the multiplicity of poetic responses to reflect on the mind itself, to wonder about its impressionability, its subjectivity, and its egocentricism. While poet Kiti of the house of Kiti Mugalana Mala writes in verse 32 "What mystery keeps me awake in my lonely bed?"

32. ම සොව නිව ඇ මෙසෙයි දුදුළ සෙල අඩදරිහි
විසිය යහඅසරට නු කිම නිඳ නො ගිය යහනෙයි

Ma sova niva ä meseyi d[u]d[u]ḷa-sela aḍadarihi
Visiya yaha-asaraṭa nu kima ninda no giya yahaneyi

(It is) indeed for happy companionship that she, having assuaged my grief, dwelt in this manner at the edge of the fortress rock. (But) why did (I) not go to sleep in (my) bed?

Another poet writes:

77. තමහට නො දිස් වූ මෙන් වෙ (ද) සිත ජනෙන (තම)
දිසෙයි නැගෙන බඳු සිකි (අ)බුරෙහි කිමිඳි සෙ තහට

Tamahaṭa no dis vū men ve (da) sita janne (tama)
Diseyi nägena bandu siki (a)burehi kimindi se tahaṭa

Is it not in the manner that (a thing) has appeared to one's self that one's mind cognizes (it)? What (appears to me) like rising up appears to you, (my) friend, as if it has dived in the sky.

One visitor even begs pardon of the ladies; not wishing to be too disturbed, he says "I will go away without thinking of you. When I go swiftly away without lingering, my mind too will not linger here."

80. මෙ නො ජත්වි නු අ සි[ටි] මිලැසි ලි විසබ නම [තා]
සුක ලද දෑ[කැ] සිවි [දැ]නා [නැ]ත විසබ තා ආ විට

Me no jat vi nu a s[iṭi] miläsi li visaba nama [tā]
Suka lada dä[kä] sivi [da]nā [nä]ta visaba tā ā v[i]ṭa

'Ah! This (manner of) standing of yours, O deer-eyed damsel, is indeed (that) of not having known the (very) name of intimacy.' 'Having seen (my) smile, pleasure has been received by (other) people. When you come (you say that there is) no intimacy (in me).'

The poets themselves make use of allusion and image to achieve memorable utterances: a famous poem by Agboy reads:

334 නිල්ක[ට්]රොළ මලෙකැ ඇවුණු වැට්කොළ මල සෙය්
සැඳැගැ සිහි වෙන්නෙය් මහනෙල්වන [හ]ය් රන්වන හුන්

Nil-ka[ṭ]roḷa malekä ävuṇu väṭkoḷa mala sey
Sändägä sihi venne-y mahanel-vana [ha]y ran-vana hun

Like a vatkola flower entangled in a blue katrola flower, the golden-coloured one who stood together with the lily-coloured one will be remembered at the advent of the evening.

Paranavitana in Sigiri Graffiti highlights the image of a *vatakolu* flower, which is yellow in colour entangled with a blue *katarolu* flower as a poetic comparison of a fair maiden, standing by the side of a dark girl.

This poem also illustrates how mood can vary in relation to season and time of day.

The decipherment of symbols and the efforts at identification can be exciting for the historian or the archaeologist. But the poets transcend the limiting frames of theory and history, perceiving in the paintings the creative embodiment of the eternal feminine mystique, while enrapturing us with the nectar of song.

NOTES